OUR ROSE-COLORED GLASSES

LEARN ABOUT THE INVISIBLE WOUNDS FROM MENTAL AND EMOTIONAL ABUSE HIDDEN BEHIND CLOSED DOORS, THE IMPORTANCE OF SPEAKING UP AND SHIFTING OLD BELIEF SYSTEMS, AND 10 TIPS TO BEGIN YOUR OWN HEALING JOURNEY AND PIVOT YOUR PAIN INTO PASSION

VICTORIA ALERCIA, LPC

Printed in the United States of America

Published in Hellertown, PA

Cover design by Anna Magruder

Cover photograph by Victoria Alercia

Author photographs by Carolina Fernandes Photography

Library of Congress Control Number: 2022915360

ISBN 978-1-958711-14-9

2 4 6 8 10 9 7 5 3 1

For more information or to place bulk orders, contact the author or Jennifer@BrightCommunications.net.

To every individual who has ever chosen to go on a healing journey, vulnerable and broken, in hopes of healing their unresolved wounds to live the rest of their life in a healthier way

To every individual who ever had the strength to speak up about domestic violence or to leave an abusive relationship, please don't ever forget the incredible amount of strength that you have. Please always remember your worth, despite the people who have chosen not to believe you or who have tried to keep you down. You deserve every amazing moment that comes into your life.

"There are wounds that never show on the body that are deeper and more hurtful than anything that bleeds."

—Laurell K. Hamilton

CONTENTS

AUTHOR'S NOTE

This book is based upon my education and experiences. I present tips here as options. My perspective is not the only way.

The information in the book can be heavy. I encourage you to take breaks, deep breaths, and time to process. This is not easy as most healing journeys are challenging, but please know this book was written from a place of love and my hope is that every reader can have the ability to hear my heart in it. I believe that our healing journeys are endless as we are all lifelong students. Please try to be patient and kind to yourself as you take that next small step forward. And know that you are never alone. Someone is praying and wanting the best for you at this very moment.

INTRODUCTION: MY WHY

I was told that I viewed the world through rose-colored glasses. It was true.

It's not that I was trying to dismiss or ignore the bad things that were happening in my world, but I wanted to make a conscious effort to choose to see the beauty in our world despite the things that went wrong. I wanted to have hope and faith. I wanted to spread love and kindness.

In my practice, I didn't work with one particular specialty population. However, over the years, I began seeing a pattern of concerns that were being presented in my office: signs of domestic violence. As I professionally and personally became more invested in navigating the difficult journey through domestic violence, it became apparent to me that many people were choosing to wear their rose-colored glasses and dismiss domestic violence that's hidden behind our closed doors.

I'm proud of my continuing education and my desire to want to learn more to understand how we operate as humans. I don't have all the answers. What I do know is it's not okay to allow domestic violence to continue. Seeing, hearing, and feeling the pain that occurs from all forms of abuse have become too much. We should all be concerned. Perhaps some people believe that domestic violence only affects the individuals in the home it's happening in. Therefore, they feel justified in keeping it a secret. However, what happens when those individuals leave their homes? What people or environment do they impact from their experience? Perhaps we are all only as healthy as our deepest unresolved wound.

Two of my favorite quotes come to mind.

> **_"Our lives begin to end the day we become silent about things that matter."_**
> **_—Martin Luther King Jr_**

> **_"Do the best you can until you know better. Then, when you know better, do better."_**
> **_—Maya Angelou_**

What matters to me? Large scale: the health and safety of our entire community. Small scale: the health and safety of my children—of all children. Children are innocent bystanders to the unhealthiness of the adults and the environment around them.

How do we change our world? By showing the younger generation a healthier way of living, speaking, acting, and communicating. We all deserve to live in a safe world—one that's full of love, not hate, and full of compassion, not judgement.

My concern is: What happens when a child lives in a home where there is constant fighting, cursing, anger, fear, and anxiety? How does that child learn how to thrive in a healthy way? By having healthy people and environments outside of the home show them a different, healthier perspective.

Before going further, I'd like to define: What is domestic violence?

Domestic violence comes from a belief system that tells the abusive person that they have the right to control another person and that they are justified in using whatever means necessary to maintain that control.

I think generations before us had many reasons, ways, and maybe even excuses to justify what happened inside their homes. They might have rationalized, "This is what our family has always done." Or, "That's just how he/she is." Or, "Well, they are family, so I have to be in their lives."

It's so incredibly important for all of us to recognize and acknowledge which thoughts we choose to focus on and more importantly, what belief systems we choose to live by.

Why? Because we all have the ability to change our belief systems. I think the unfortunate reality is that it has become much easier for people to believe a lie and continue toxic, damaging lifestyles, instead of considering a truth that would require them to turn inward and change their belief systems. We live in a world that wants things simple and with instant gratification.

Nothing about domestic violence is simple.

It is important to acknowledge that we impact each other more than we know. We are connected as humanity. The choices we make impact the people living in our homes, and our choices also impact many people outside of our homes as well.

Perpetuators of domestic violence often have the mentality that it is okay to harm other people just as long as it stays hidden in their homes and also that it is okay to manipulate and control another person by fear. That is a very damaging belief system to live by.

But what if those people were asked, "Was there a moment in your life that you felt scared, out of control, or unloved? Was there a time when your needs were not being met?" If we could help these people uncover their wounds in a safe environment, to guide them to a healing space, would that be enough to save our families and relationships?

What if we could acknowledge that we are all wounded and flawed?

This approach doesn't dismiss that abuse is wrong. There should still be consequences, but what if there was also rehabilitation? What if we as a community were able to approach a concern with understanding and compassion instead of shame, judgement, and criticism to all parties involved. In that environment, perhaps abusers might be more open to seeking help.

Contrary to popular belief, domestic violence is not a man-verses-woman concern. Current statistics show that 1 in 4 women and 1 in 7 men are involved in domestic violence. Most people understand that it's difficult for a woman to speak up, but how much more difficult would it be for a man to speak up about being abused by a woman? If society stereotypes a man to have to be strong, I can only imagine the amount of shame that could potentially be placed on a man for speaking up.

If we want to change our world, let's teach and show each other healthier ways of thinking, acting, communicating, and living. Never underestimate the power of planting the seed of positive change. We can start now.

My hope is that by reading this book, people who lived through or are currently living in domestic violence will feel less alone. I also hope that people who read this book with an open mind might consider shifting their old belief systems and healing themselves to help guide younger generations to a healthier way of living.

Along with the guidance of a few of my community connections, this book will light a path to show how you can speak up about your circumstances, understand the dynamics of a narcissistic relationship, find the courage to break the cycle, strengthen your spirituality, and learn tips to use on your own healing journey.

We sometimes think we want to disappear, but all we really want is to be found.

ONE

BE HUMAN AND ASK FOR HELP

> *"Tell your story.*
> *Shout it. Write it.*
> *Whisper it if you have to.*
> *But tell it.*
> *Some won't understand it.*
> *Some will outright reject it.*
> *But many will thank you for it.*
> *And then the most magical thing will happen.*
> *One by one, your tribe will gather.*
> *And you will never feel alone again."*
> *—L.R. Knost*

I recognize now that one of my old belief systems was that I wanted to be superwoman. When other people viewed me as a wife, mother, business owner, volunteer, and also someone who was still able to bake cookies for the PTA, I loved being viewed as the woman who could do it all.

But I realized that I was becoming completely drained. Depleted. Exhausted. I had an expectation of myself that I could do everything for everyone and do it all well, without needing a break or to ask for help.

For years, I tried to be my own therapist and to be the therapist of my home. I had the education and experience. I thought, *Why shouldn't I be able to fix the problems in my home?*

At one point, I even shamed myself, questioning whether I was a good therapist. I saw myself helping the people and couples who came into my office, but I feared that I couldn't help myself.

Does any of this sound like you?

When a person is living in domestic violence, one can feel shame, as well as depression, anxiety, and low self-esteem. You might feel trapped, overwhelmed, and alone.

If you're reading this and recognize some of your own story in these words, you might think, *I no longer want to live like this, but I don't know how to change things.* Often in domestic violence situations, a person might not have proof that anything is wrong. Or they might justify the abuse in their own mind, thinking, *It's not bad all of the time.* Or they might worry, *If I choose to speak up, who will believe me?* It's very important to understand that fear is a prominent aspect to domestic violence. It's a catch 22: There is fear in staying, and there is also fear in leaving.

Bruises and scars from physical abuse are visible, easy to see. However, the bruises and scars from emotional, mental, psychological, and narcissistic abuse are invisible, and they might seem impossible to understand or identify.

How do you obtain proof for those invisible wounds? I believe that's part of the barrier of healing from domestic violence.

But the truth is: A narcissistic abuser can even try to dismiss physical wounds by blaming the victim for falling or being clumsy. Even physical abuse can be defended, dismissed, and lied about. If abuse is difficult to prove *with* physical evidence, you can imagine how difficult it is to prove *without* physical evidence.

It feels scary to choose to speak up about domestic violence. Specifically, it's frightening when you are speaking up about a person who appears to have mastered the ability to manipulate those around you. When someone no longer has the ability to control you, they might attempt to control the people around you instead. This can include them reversing roles and telling a story that puts them in the victim role. They might never, not evenly slightly, indicate their faults of what they have done. This is painful. This scenario adds to the trauma of the people who lived in domestic violence with that person.

There is something important to consider when there are children in a violent home. A parent's natural instinct should be to protect the children. If you are protecting the children, then how are you getting the proof in that moment of what is happening? It's sad that you might feel like you have to override your natural instinct of protecting your child to grab your phone and record a video to have proof.

But what happens while we are waiting for proof?

The abuse and trauma continue to occur, and studies show long-term damage of psychological abuse. Here are some child statistics from the national domestic violence hotline.

• Children witnessed violence in nearly 1 in 4 (22 percent) of intimate partner violence cases filed in state courts.

• 30 to 60 percent of intimate partner violence perpetrators also abuse children in the household.

• 40 percent of child abuse victims also report experiencing domestic violence.

Here are more sobering statistics.

• One study found that children exposed to violence in the home were 15 times more likely to be physically and/or sexually assaulted than the national average.

• According to the US Advisory Board on Child Abuse and Neglect, domestic violence might be the single major precursor to fatalities from child abuse and neglect in the United States.

• Intimate partner violence alone affects more than 12 million people every year.

• Almost half of all women and men in the United States have experienced psychological aggression by an intimate partner in their lifetime (48.4 percent and 48.8 percent, respectively).

• The National Commission on Covid-19 and criminal justice shows an increase in the United States by a little over 8 percent, following the imposition of lockdown orders during 2020.

• *The American Journal of Emergency Medicine* reported that domestic violence cases increased by 25 to 33 percent globally.

I assume that perhaps these numbers are actually higher than documented because the fear of speaking up is so high. Many people still live in secret with domestic violence.

I don't think a major barrier is the lack of proof. I think a barrier is the lack of understanding of how difficult it is to obtain proof and also the number of people who still choose to dismiss the severity of what is occurring.

My own rose-colored glasses led me to believe that we wouldn't or shouldn't need proof of domestic violence in order to be believed and then to receive help for all involved.

But then, I learned how to look *over* my own rose-colored glasses to finally see.

Here's what I discovered.

The old beliefs from some families and community around me:

•You should never get divorced.

•You stay together for the children.

•You never talk about what happens behind your closed doors.

...all these choices can lead to damaging, long-lasting wounds and trauma.

The new beliefs:

• Prioritize your own mental, emotional, and physical welfare. This is not being selfish. But in an abusive relationship, you might be ignoring your own needs.

• Sometimes divorce is the healthier option, even for the kids. When deciding whether to stay or leave, consider the example of a relationship you're showing your children. If you are showing them a relationship where you are called names, hit, having things broken, experiencing constant fighting, feeling scared, and being disrespected, you are showing your children it's okay for them to be in that relationship as well. You are teaching your kids the wrong thing about love. If the relationship you are in is something you wouldn't ever want for your children, why would you want it for yourself?

I'm aware that choosing to leave is an extremely difficult decision to make. I'm aware how much fear there is in the choice to stay and in the choice to leave. But consider what a beautiful feeling it is on the other side to be able to tell your children and show them that they matter and that they deserve to be only around people who respect them and treat them kindly. By choosing to leave, you are showing your worth and your children's worth.

• It's healthy to have safe experts and friends to confide in. I believe that keeping things hidden can feel shameful, which is one of the most difficult emotions connected to suffering and trauma. The unfortunate reality is even if you are truly able to show your vulnerability, someone might still shame, criticize, and judge you. But by speaking up, you are showing your humanness, breaking the silence, and revealing the wounds that need to be healed—probably from generations of a family dynamic.

Before you judge me, step into my shoes and walk the life I am living, and if you get as far as I am, then maybe you will see how strong I really am.

Where Can You Ask for Help?

I'm a firm believer in the importance of practicing what you preach. One of the best pieces of advice I received in graduate school was when a professor encouraged our class to seek our own therapy before becoming licensed therapists. I'm proud to say that I experienced my own healing as a client for many years before becoming a therapist, and I still currently work with my own therapist.

There is no shame in acknowledging that you are human, and even that you struggle. I believe one of the qualities that makes me a genuine therapist is showing my humanness to my clients. I practice ethical self-disclosure, and I will share with a client that I have struggled with my own depression, anxiety, and self-critical thinking—as it pertains to their healing journey. Sometimes, I think perhaps we can underestimate the amount of resources that are actually accessible to help us when we are struggling. In these moments, it's helpful to acknowledge how we might be our own barriers to healing. It's completely understandable that it can feel scary to speak up to ask for help to begin with. I acknowledge how scary the step of admitting you need help can be. Sometimes the step that seems scariest is the step you need to take the most. Change is difficult in the beginning and messy in the middle, but it has the potential to be beautiful in the end. Even though you might feel alone at the first step, please believe that many people want to help and see you succeed in developing a heathier life for yourself.

If you need help, therapy is a good place to start. Check out www. psychologytoday.com, where you can search a database for licensed therapists in your area and view their profiles to find the best fit for your healing journey.

Unfortunately, barriers can come up, such as not having insurance or having a high deductible. If that's the case for you, look into local shelters or domestic violence organizations. There's also a free national domestic violence hotline: visit www.thehotline.com, call 1-800-799-SAFE (7233), or text "START" to 88788.

If you choose to reach out to family or friends for support, trust your intuition on whether or not they are truly able to hold space for you.

> *"What does it mean to hold space for another person? It means that we are willing to walk alongside another person in whatever journey they're on without judging them, making them feel inadequate, trying to fix them, or trying to impact the outcome. When we hold space for other people, we open our hearts, offer unconditional support, and let go of judgment and control."*
> *—Heather Platt*

One of the challenges that I think we can face during our healing journey is identifying the people in our lives who are able to hold space for us. I think a common thought process is that our family and friends should be our biggest support system. Discerning who to invite into your support system will greatly affect the direction of your healing.

If you currently have someone in your life who is still living in trauma or who has left a traumatic situation, please be careful how you respond to them. Even if you have also been in an abusive relationship or have also gone through a divorce, you have not been in their exact situation.

Some phrases can be hurtful, such as, "What doesn't kill you makes your stronger." A traumatic situation may have not killed someone, but it could have left them shaking, disassociated, sleepless, and trustless and broken their sense of safety. We don't want to stay stuck in our trauma, but we also don't want it downplayed. Be mindful of the facts of that person's experience, and if you don't know the facts, ask. If you hear two different stories, consider that both might be true.

What Can You Expect When You Ask for Help?

One would hope everyone will be patient, kind, and supportive, especially when you ask for help. But people don't always know what to say, and sometimes they say exactly the opposite of what you need to hear.

I believe that when we're in a place of pain, it becomes more difficult to not react or take things personally from other people around us. People might say to you that you are playing the martyr, that you need to stop acting like a victim, or that you should just stop speaking up. You might feel very hurt.

If that happens to you, I encourage a pause and deep breaths.

Once you step away, you can consider these perspectives: Sometimes a person's words or behavior has nothing to do with you, but instead it is a reflection of their own unresolved wounds. Perhaps something you were speaking up about triggered that person to respond to you in that way. Try to understand their responses and try to hear helping in their words. You ultimately might decide that what is best for you at this time is to set boundaries. Remind yourself that your story matters. However, sometimes it's healthy to take a pause first and be aware of who or what environment you are speaking up in. Not everyone will be ready or welcoming to hear what you have to say. That doesn't mean that you go silent. Instead, that means that you take time to heal and adjust your boundaries and support system accordingly.

> **Your story is the key that can unlock someone else's prison. Share your testimony.**

It's important to know that recovering from domestic violence is not something you can do alone. I strongly recommend reaching out to a provider who specializes in understanding domestic violence, narcissistic abuse, or whatever situation you are facing. Some abusers can be very manipulative, When I work with domestic violence survivors, many of them ask me, "Am I crazy?"

Even though I have 10 years of college education and 15 years of experience as a therapist, I still question myself when in the presence of someone with narcissistic traits. On my journey, sometimes I needed reassurance that I wasn't crazy. One of my resources during my educational and healing journey was Aaron Myers, PsyD, a clinical and forensics psychologist, who assisted me in removing my rose-colored glasses with my skewed perception of domestic violence.

~

Expert Q&A: Aaron Myers, PsyD

Aaron Myers, PsyD, is a licensed psychologist who works for Valliere & Counseling Associates. He specializes in forensic and clinical psychology. Dr. Myers specifically provides evaluation and treatment to sexual and violent offenders as well as people who have experienced emotional, psychological, physical, and sexual abuse. He has testified as an expert witness in several local counties. Also, he treats people who have other common mental health issues, such as depression, anxiety, trauma, and relationship problems. Additionally, Dr. Myers has presented trainings on a variety of topics related to his specialty, including violence and abuse dynamics, narcissism, and accountability.

How do you define an abuser?

An individual who targets and is intentional with their behavior toward someone to maintain power and control.

What are the current statistics of someone being abused today?

Abuse definitely increased, considering the state of our world. There was no way to get away from perpetrators during the Covid-19 pandemic.

Do abused people become abusers?

There is a perception that there is a cycle of abuse. Some people might assume that the abused become abusers. However, if someone who was abused knows how bad it feels, why would they abuse someone else? The majority of people who are abused do not go on to abuse others.

What are some common traits, behaviors, or red flags of an abuser?

A perpetrator is typically someone who feels entitled and wants to control others. They feel that their behaviors toward others are justified despite the context or circumstances. Nothing will modify their perception. When someone feels entitled, they view themselves as the most important person. How they feel and what they want trumps anything and anyone else. How bad narcissism and abuse can get depends on the importance of the perpetrators self-image. Image can play a role, especially duplicitous behavior. Perpetrators are often concerned about how they appear to others. This helps them to maintain control of the people they want and to minimize the chances of being held accountable or reported. If they are more concerned about their public image, they will keep the abuse closeted. They desperately try to keep their victims isolated so no one sees what is happening. There are then less people to control.

When a victim speaks up about domestic violence that was hidden behind closed doors and the response received was, "But he/she was always nice to me," it's important to understand that "niceness" can be used as a weapon against a victim. Niceness in public is socially acceptable, but it doesn't show anything about an individual's real personality or deeper issues. An individual can appear nice yet not have any empathy or boundaries—but plenty of aggression. When an individual isn't capable of having empathy, it means that they don't care about someone else's well-being, thoughts, or feelings. Some perpetrators have empathy, but they use it to exploit the other person because now they know the other person's thoughts/feelings. To have compassion means that you are able to look out for another's best interest. Empathy can be beneficial. It depends on how it is used. A perpetrator can use empathy as a means to exploit and take on the role of a victim, which makes it more difficult for the actual victim to speak up for help.

How does a person become abusive?

It all stems from their thought processes. First, violence and abuse have to be viewed as acceptable options to them. The second is their personality characteristic: They have to believe the target deserved the abuse in some way. They believe that their behaviors are justified, and they believe that the target deserved to be treated badly. If the victim didn't do what the abuser wanted them to do, they feel they are justified to treat them any way they want.

Is it possible for a spouse/family/friends/community to rehabilitate an abuser?

Accountability is the only way to get a perpetrator help. A perpetrator is typically an individual who wants power and control. They have a need to dominate the situation. They feel entitled to deserve something that they haven't earned. They perceive themselves as superior. They feel justified to devalue and disrespect others. They focus on their good public image. They want to be perceived in a positive light. They gain their power and control by manipulating others and grooming others to do what they want. They are known to twist things around. Abusers can be very calculating in what they say.

If an abuser is surrounded by individuals who mirror and support their abusive behavior, they remain stuck in that damaging, distorted viewpoint, and they can even doubt their own intuition. Families will conform to abusive behaviors and believe that the distorted thought process is okay, many times to appease the abuser.

If an individual's mind is made up, they are choosing to believe that abuse is okay, then the method that the family chooses to try to implement won't help.

Marriage counseling doesn't help because it requires both parties to hold themselves responsible for their actions, and it assumes both parties are responsible for the issues. An abuser will often view themselves above their spouse. Sometimes it is difficult for a victim to even see their abuser from an accurate perspective. You can even find yourself justifying their behaviors. If they don't check all the boxes of a common abuser, then you might not want to identify them as one.

An abuser feels their rights are greater than their partner and/or children's rights. Think of three circles representing rights. In an abusive situation, the abuser's circle is much bigger than the others. In a healthy relationship, everyone's circle is the same size.

If an abuser does seek treatment, how can we tell if changes are real?

The individual has to fully acknowledge and understand that what they have done is wrong and be able to accept the consequences that may come along with this, such as people might be mad at them, they can't still blame the victim, they can't tell other people that they have to get over it, and they can't tell others when they should have forgiven him/her. The abuser should continue to show longer term effort and commitment.

It's important that we understand that change can be very complex, and there is a lot that goes into someone changing their behaviors. When you are in a relationship with someone who is abusive, continuing to hold on to hope can blind you from what is actually happening.

For the changes to stay, family and friends need to hold the abuser accountable for their actions, and the abuser should be open to their feedback.

Why is it so difficult for victims to heal?

It's so important to pay attention to your own intuition and feelings. One of the best ways for a victim to heal is to find specialized, professional help so they can be educated and help in the processing of the stereotype of what an abuser is, rather than the monster in your head and what you experienced. A visual can be helpful with this to show victims a spectrum of where their abuser lies between someone who is violent and someone who is healthy.

It's also important to acknowledge that multiple things can be true at the same time. For example, your spouse can do good things as a father and partner, and also still beat you. Your spouse can be helpful with paying the bills, and still call you names and devalue you. In these instances and in many more, the good quality of the individual does not outweigh the poor treatment. Abuse is still not right.

What other points are important for readers to know about abusers and victims?

When a victim speaks up about domestic violence, one of the biggest fears is that they won't be believed. Here are a few reasons why someone might choose not to believe a victim: A bystander might not want to disconfirm their own personal experiences that they obtained with the accused. This puts them in a place where they might have to question their own intuition and why they were wrong. It is easier for someone to believe the public image that has been viewed of someone than to question themselves and consider an alternative view. If they choose to believe the victim, they would now be in a position where they would have to hold the abuser accountable.

When a victim speaks up, the outsiders have a choice. They can choose to maintain the same relationship with the abuser and deny the new information that has been shared, which appears to be the easier route to take on the surface. Or the outsiders can integrate the new information and enter a state of grief and loss along with the victim. They would be grieving the loss of the individual who they thought they knew.

The easier path is to allow the abuser to manipulate them in believing his/her version of the situation. Everyone is responsible for their own well-being. However, if an individual clings to a rigid view, boundaries need to be implemented. Many individuals still operate from a black-and-white perspective, but much of our world is gray.

What resources do you recommend for people who are trying to heal from trauma?

- *Why Does He Do That?*, *When Dad Hurts Mom* by Lundy Bancroft
- *Should I Stay or Should I Go?* By Ramani Durvasula
- *Understanding Victims of Interpersonal Violence* by Veronique N. Valliere

The Man in the Arena, by Theodore Roosevelt

"It is not the critic who counts; not the man who points out how the strong man stumbles, or where the doer of deeds could have done them better. The credit belongs to the man who is actually in the arena, whose face is marred by dust and sweat and blood; who strives valiantly; who errs, who comes short again and again, because there is no effort without error and shortcoming; but who does actually strive to do the deeds; who knows great enthusiasms, the great devotions; who spends himself in a worthy cause; who at the best knows in the end the triumph of high achievement, and who at the worst, if he fails, at least fails while daring greatly, so that his place shall never be with those cold and timid souls who neither know victory nor defeat."

The powerful quote resonated with Brene Brown, PhD, a research professor at the University of Houston Graduate Course of Social Work, who gave the blockbuster TEDTalks: Brene Brown: The Power of Vulnerability and Brene Brown: Listening to Shame. In the introduction to her book, she riffed on Roosevelt's words, which she said perfectly encapsulated her research into why we find being vulnerable such a hard thing to do. "When we spend our lives waiting until we're perfect or bulletproof before we walk into the arena, we ultimately sacrifice relationships and opportunities that may not be recoverable, we squander our precious time, and we turn our backs on our gifts, those unique contributions that only we can make. Perfect and and bulletproof are seductive, but they don't exist in the human experience.

"If you're not in the arena getting your butt kicked on occasion, I am not interested in or open to your feedback. There are a million cheap seats in the world today filled with people who will never be brave with their own lives but will spend every ounce of energy they have hurling advice and judgment at those of us trying to dare greatly. Their only contributions are criticism, cynicism, and fear-mongering. If you're criticizing from a place where you're not putting yourself on the line, I'm not interested in your feedback."

After meeting with Dr. Myers, I purchased the book *Why Does He Do That?*

Have you ever read a book and thought, *I am going to highlight the parts of the book that really speak to me,* then you end up highlighting the whole book? I'll share a few main points for me, then I encourage you to purchase the book to read the rest.

"At moments, he sounds wounded and lost, hungering for love and for someone to take care of him. When this side of him emerges, he appears open and ready to heal. He seems to let down his guard, his hard exterior softens, and he may take on the quality of a hurt child, difficult and frustrating but lovable. Looking at him in this deflated state, his partner had trouble imagining that the abuser inside of him will ever be back. The beast that takes him over at other times looks completely unrelated to the tender person she now sees."

When some people have a serious problem, like abusers, they might work hard at keeping it hidden. Abuse is a problem that lies entirely within the abuser.

The problem is that an issue cannot be confronted if it continues to be remained hidden. The better we understand abusers, the more we can create homes and relationships that are havens of love and safety, as they should be. Peace should begin at home.

Here are some myths about abusers.

- They were abused as a child.
- They were hurt in their previous relationship.
- They abuse the people they love the most.
- They hold their feelings in too much.
- They have an aggressive personality.
- They are mentally ill.
- They have low self-esteem.
- They are afraid of intimacy and abandonment.
- They have poor communication and conflict resolution skills.
- They abuse drugs and alcohol.

Here are some realities about abusers.

- They are controlling.
- They feel entitled.
- They twist things into their opposites.
- They disrespect their partner and considers themselves superior.
- They confuse love and abuse.
- They are manipulative.
- They strive to have a good public image.
- They feel justified.
- They deny and minimize their abuse toward others.
- They are possessive.

If any of this sounds familiar to you, please know this: You are NOT crazy! Abusers are often unwilling to be non-abusive. They choose to not give up power and control. Put your time and energy into healing yourself and learning how to trust and love yourself again.

There is ALWAYS a way to save ourselves!

One day, you will tell your story of how you've overcome what you are going through now, and it will become part of someone else's survival guide.

TWO

THE NARCISSISTIC FAMILY DYNAMIC

> *"When you stand up in front of the whole world unafraid*
> *to express your truth, you clear an easier path for others to*
> *do the same."*
> *—Stacie Martin*

As we begin talking about family dynamics of abuse, here are some definitions it's important to understand.

•*Verbal abuse* is a type of psychological/mental abuse that involves the use of oral, gestured, and written language directed to a victim. Verbal abuse can include harassing, labeling, insulting, scolding, rebuking, or excessive yelling toward a person.

•*Mental abuse* is meant to undermine your self-esteem and make you feel worse about yourself. It is also a form of manipulation and control. The effects of mental abuse are just as detrimental as the effects of physical abuse.

•*Emotional abuse* involves nonphysical behavior that belittles another person and can include insults, put-downs, verbal threats, or other tactics that make the victim feel threatened, inferior, ashamed, or degraded.

•***Narcissistic abuse*** includes all of the above—mental, emotional, and verbal. It is a type of emotional abuse where the abuser only cares about themselves and uses words and actions to manipulate their partner's behavior and emotional state. Effects of narcissistic abuse can vary, depending on how long one has endured these types of relationships.

Although these forms don't leave physical wounds, they all leave *invisible* wounds. They don't come with visible "proof" of the pain, which makes it that much more difficult for someone to speak up to receive help for it. It's difficult to be believed unless a person is educated, trained on the topic, or lived through a similar situation themselves.

These forms of traumatic abuse leave long-lasting negative effects on people. You can work though healing, but it takes a lot of effort and an amazing support system. Education is key. Being open and willing to learn, understand, change, and help is crucial to our community healing.

Have you heard the term "narcissistic personality disorder"? It's becoming more talked about. It is a mental condition in which people have an inflated sense of their own importance, a deep need for attention and admiration, and a lack of empathy for others. It often leads to very troubled relationships. Behind the narcissist's mask of extreme confidence lies a fragile self-esteem that's vulnerable to the slightest criticism.

A narcissistic personality disorder causes problems in many areas of life, such as relationships and work, school, or finances. People with narcissistic personality disorder might be visibly unhappy and disappointed when they're not given the admiration and attention that they believe they deserve. They may find their relationships unfulfilling. Other people might not like to spend time with them.

Here are some signs of narcissistic personality disorder.

- An exaggerated sense of self-importance
- A sense of entitlement

- Need for constant, excessive admiration
- Expectation to be recognized as superior, even if it's undeserved
- Inflated talents and achievements
- Preoccupation with fantasies about success and power
- Obsessively seek beauty or the perfect mate
- Belief they are superior and can only associate with equally special people
- Monopolize conversations
- Belittle people they perceive as inferior
- Expect special favors
- Resist questioning of their expectations
- Take advantage of others to get what they want
- Have an inability or unwillingness to recognize the needs and feelings of others
- Be envious of others and believe others envy them
- Act arrogant and seem conceited, boastful, and pretentious
- Insist on the best of everything

At the same time, people with narcissistic personality disorder have trouble handling anything they perceive as criticism, and they can:

- Become impatient or angry when they don't receive special treatment
- Have significant interpersonal problems and easily feel slighted
- React with rage or contempt
- Belittle the other person to make themselves appear superior
- Have difficulty regulating emotions and behavior
- Experience major problems dealing with stress and adapting to change
- Feel depressed and moody because they fall short of perfection
- Have secret feelings of insecurity, shame, vulnerability and humiliation

What causes narcissistic personality disorder? We don't know. It's likely complex. Narcissistic personality disorder may be linked to:

- **Genetics:** inherited characteristics
- **Environment:** mismatches in parent-child relationships with either excessive adoration or excessive criticism that is poorly attuned to the child's experience
- **Neurobiology:** the connection between the brain and behavior and thinking

In a narcissistic family, the needs of the parents are the focus, and the children are expected to meet those needs. The healthy family model is turned on its head to support the parents rather than to foster the children's development.

As in other kinds of dysfunctional families, there is abuse and corresponding denial of the abuse. There is also secrecy, neglect, unrealistic expectations, lack of empathy, disrespect for boundaries, and ongoing conflict.

Here are some signs a person might be in a narcissistic family.

- Acceptance is conditional.
- Submission is required.
- Someone must be blamed for problems.
- Vulnerability is dangerous.
- Sides must be taken.
- There is never enough love to go around.
- Feelings are wrong.

Many narcissistic families break into common patterns and roles, including the following.

Narcissist: This is the family tyrant, who everyone else tiptoes around, trying to avoid criticism and conflict. It's usually a parent, but it could be a child/sibling.

A person with narcissistic personality disorder (NPD) experiences disrupted attachment with caregivers early in life that impedes healthy emotional development. The child is unable to establish a secure sense of identity, resilient self-esteem, or an empathetic connection with others, making him/her emotionally unstable, self-focused, delusional, demanding, and often stunningly callous and cruel.

As parents, narcissists invert the parent-child relationship by putting their needs before those of their children. They may be neglectful, engulfing, exploitative, and/or outright abusive.

Codependent: Codependent enablers support narcissists by unquestionably accepting their larger-than-life persona, complying with their narrative about the family, and cleaning up their messes. Narcissists typically manipulate enablers through alternating abuse and special treatment. Enablers are perpetually avoiding attack while also seeking rewards such as affection, praise, or money. The enabler is often under the delusion that she or he is the only one who can truly understand the narcissist and meet his or her needs. Enablers commonly experience trauma bonding with the narcissist, becoming emotionally and physically addicted to codependent abuse cycles. The primary enabler in the narcissistic family is usually a partner/spouse, but it might be a parent or child.

Flying monkeys: Often one or more children or other relatives in the narcissistic family, flying monkeys are enablers who also perpetrate the narcissist's abuse on targeted victims. They are the most manipulative members of the family, and in fact they might become narcissists themselves. They assist in the narcissist's dirty work and carry out abuse by proxy.

Golden child: The golden child is the narcissist parent's idealized favorite, bestowed with special status. The narcissist projects what he or she wants to believe about himself or herself onto this child and engulfs the child's identity into her/his own. Roles and rules in the narcissistic family are fluid and changeable, and the narcissist parent may reassign the part of golden child to another if it suits his/her shifting moods and motives or if family circumstances change.

Scapegoat: The child targeted as the scapegoat functions as a projection screen for the narcissist's self-hatred, rage, and disappointments. Blamed for family problems, this child is fair game for abuse from flying monkeys, too. Oftentimes the scapegoat is different from the family culture in some way. This child may be the strongest, most aware, and/or most empathetic child, the one who questions the family system and perhaps stands up to the narcissist in defense of others. Unlike the golden child, the scapegoat is least invested in upholding the family system because she or he recognizes its injustice and benefits least from it.

Here are some terms pertaining to a narcissistic family dynamic.

Gaslighting: This is a form of psychological abuse that involves undermining another person's mental state by leading them to question their perceptions of reality. The narcissistic manipulator uses denial, dismissal, distortion, and other forms of lying to erode victims' belief in their own judgment and, ultimately, their sanity. The term comes from the 1944 Hollywood film *Gaslight,* a classic depiction of this kind of brainwashing.

Narcissistic rage: A defining feature of the narcissistic personality is emotional instability and reactivity, including hair-trigger rage about anything perceived as a threat to his/her inflated sense of entitlement. Far beyond normal anger, narcissistic rage is terrifying, and it can include physical violence. It can be overt or cloaked in passive-aggressive behavior such as guilt-tripping or silent treatment.

Narcissistic supply: Like a parasite, the narcissistic personality is highly dependent on others for emotional sustenance, demanding continuous attention, agreement, and adoration. Anyone the narcissist can exploit—a partner, child, relative, employee, student, or friend—is a potential source of supply. Without others to manipulate and draw validation from, the narcissist is an empty husk.

Projection: We all project from time to time, but the narcissist does so unawarely and compulsively. When narcissists project, they beam their thoughts and feelings onto others so they don't have to take responsibility or carry painful emotions. Because they lack self-awareness and don't respect boundaries, narcissists project as a matter of course in all their relationships. If the narcissist lied, you are the liar; if he or she is childish, you are immature; if he or she insulted you, you are critical; if he or she demanded reassurance, you are insecure; if he or she ate food off your plate, you are a selfish pig.

Hoovering: Because narcissists are so completely self-centered, they ultimately make people around them unhappy and eventually drive many people away. If a source of supply pulls away or tries to go no contact, the narcissist may attempt to hoover (as in vacuum-suck) them back within his/her realm of control.

Diagnosis and Treatment

I cringe when reading information about narcissism. In all my personal and professional experience with narcissism, the main statement that I have felt about myself and what I have heard others tell me numerous times is, "Am I crazy?" That is exactly what being around someone with narcissistic personality disorder does to a person. You don't know who they are. But the worst thing is when their constant manipulation makes you feel like who don't even know who you are anymore.

This is why it is so important to your mental health to set boundaries as soon as possible. You might feel like you need an incredible amount of strength to walk away from that toxicity. What makes it worse is when you finally do walk away and you see and hear continued toxicity directed toward you for leaving. If no one has told you before, I am telling you now, "YOU WERE NEVER ASKING FOR TOO MUCH BY SIMPLY ASKING TO BE RESPECTED." In my life, I have made the mistake more than once to focus too much of my time and energy on people who chose not to love me. I finally learned that it isn't personal but perhaps it shows their unresolved wounds. Healthy people should be able to acknowledge when their words and actions hurt other people, and they should also be able to show compassion and be willing to change their behavior.

I've learned to release my anger and my pain and pray for them instead. I feel sad for them. How difficult it must be to be controlled out of fear and to have to follow toxic unwritten rules instead of being able to be your true self.

This is extremely difficult to heal from. It takes time. Find your genuine healing group and lean on them. Surrounded yourself with people who remind you that you are loved, cared for, heard, seen, understood, prayed for, and deserving of respect. We all deserve that. Focus your time and energy on learning how to love yourself again.

What if an abuser apologizes? Saying "sorry" is NOT necessarily an apology. A real apology requires:

- Freely admitting fault
- Fully accepting responsibility
- Humbly asking for forgiveness
- Immediately changing behavior
- Actively rebuilding trust

It's understandable that we want to give multiple chances to those we love, but if there is no change in actions, remember: ***We teach people how to treat us based on what we are willing to tolerate.***

That means that you *don't* have to apologize for:

- Your feelings
- Having firm boundaries
- Saying no
- Being emotional

- Needing to take a break
- Asking for clarity when you don't understand
- Changing and becoming healthier
- Not settling for less than you deserve
- Healing at your own pace

~

Christina's Story

What was the most difficult part about living in a domestic violence relationship?

The domestic violence relationship I lived with was psychological/emotional. When there is constant gaslighting and someone is able to manipulate you into believing that everything that you do is wrong and take you away from anyone else who can support you, you lose yourself. They have you convinced that they are the only person who cares about you, yet they are the one who is constantly putting you down.

He caused arguments with my parents and moved me out of the city into the suburbs where I knew no one and only had him. He could completely control my environment and control me. He told me that he loved me, and then he would tell me that I'm a horrible person because I got dinner to him late because I worked all day and went to school and had to clean the kitchen before I could start cooking dinner for him, oh, and he didn't like what I made him anyway. I needed to cook what his mother makes, but I couldn't do that right either.

And he kept telling me that I couldn't do anything without him. Like that new car loan, he said he needed to be on the signature, because I couldn't qualify for that on my own—even though I could have easily, and I did when I left him and got the title in my name only. I was the one who had a sizable savings after graduating college because I had served in the Army and they paid for my degree, whereas he was in student loan debt.

Then one night, he sat me down and for I don't know how long he told me everything that was wrong with me and how no one was talking to me anymore because I was such a burden on them. He said I was a burden on everyone, including him.

I left, crying, and attempted suicide, writing an apology letter for ruining everyone's life as he had just told me I did.

The next day in the emergency room, he asked, "How could you do this to me" like he had done nothing and had not just the night before told me he didn't love me anymore because I was such a horrible burden to him. It took me another month and a half and a repeat of him telling me how horrible I was before I could choose to leave him.

What was the most difficult part about leaving a domestic violence relationship?

I had just spent the past 18 months being told that I couldn't make it on my own, so there was a lot of fear of truly failing. He wouldn't leave the home, and I couldn't afford to leave myself. I had to drop out of school to work full-time to start supporting myself.

One day, he started an argument, and I left to cool off. When I returned, the cops showed up.

Funny thing was that by the end, they were yelling at him and telling him to leave me alone since I was sleeping in the living room on an old mattress because he refused to give up the bedroom.

When he did finally move out, he purposely stole a box of my belongings to use as leverage over me. In order to get my possessions back, he wanted me to bring him the box of nice steak knives his friend gifted us at our wedding, but it had been decided that I would keep the kitchen stuff, and I paid for the wedding and that was the only nice present we had received from all of his friends he invited "because I had such a big family," and he insisted the number of invites on each side needed to be equal.

When I showed up to meet him at the title company to sign my car over to my name, he brought a police officer with him "for protection." When I told him that I was keeping the knives and went to grab the box of my belongings, the police officer stepped in and threatened me with a misdemeanor for trying to get my stuff back from him. He refused to file for divorce because he had convinced me to not file for alimony, so why pay money for the attorney. He took every piece of me. He knew I was shattered when I met him, and he abused me even further.

What guidance would you give someone who is trying to leave or heal from it?

Just get out. End it. It's not worth it. You are worthy of more than that.

It's going to take time to heal, but it will happen. You will persevere. Take your time to heal. Learn from your mistakes. Don't just keep falling into that same pattern of relationship. Learn your value. Love yourself. Love comes from within; you don't find it externally.

When you truly love yourself and feel worthy of love from others, the right person will come into your life. But you have to put in that work for yourself first.

~

Your value doesn't decrease based upon someone's inability to see your worth.

THREE

BREAKING THE CYCLE

"I spent so many years walking on eggshells…never doing or saying the right thing. One day, I decided I'd had enough and stomped all over them. Those broken eggshells cut me deeply as I walked away…but this…was the most beautiful pain I had ever felt."
—S.L. Heaton

If you grew up in a narcissistic family dynamic, you probably wonder, *How can I help the next generation?*

By helping yourself.

Understanding ourselves is probably one of the most challenging journeys that we will ever be on in our lives. I believe it is very important to look at the generations in our family before us. What did they do that seemed healthy? What did they do that seemed unhealthy?

This is where it can get messy because if someone grew up in an abusive family and home, they might think that is "normal." It's not until someone with a different perspective shows them that there might be another way of thinking or living that they understand the challenges they were living under.

I think sometimes this can be a reason why someone ends up in an abusive relationship even after they leave their childhood home. They might not know what a healthy home or relationship looks like because no one showed them or told them.

In order to break the cycle, first you need to understand the difference between healthy and unhealthy belief systems in a family dynamic.

Family does NOT mean:

- Keeping secrets
- Walking on eggshells
- Lying to keep the peace
- Pretending others are healthy when they are not
- Tiptoeing around the truth
- Attending events that derail your healing process
- Defending poor choices
- Engaging in toxic behaviors
- Remaining loyal to destructive patterns
- Sacrificing your needs in attempt to save and fix others
- Discouraging people from asking questions
- Prohibiting people from sharing family secrets
- Not admitting to faults
- Not expressing your feelings
- Focusing only on your needs and no one else's

If you didn't come from a healthy family, make sure a healthy family comes from you.

Healthy families can look like this.

- Open communication
- Feeling comfortable to be themselves
- Able to speak up about your truth

- Being able to identify problems
- Setting boundaries for your own well-being
- Acknowledging and changing unhealthy behaviors
- Remaining loyal to your own health
- Healing yourself and allowing others to do the same
- Encouraging others to ask questions in order to understand
- Allowing people to address family concerns
- Acknowledging that we are all flawed
- Responding with compassion and understanding, instead of criticism and shaming
- Considering the welfare of everyone involved

Often in a cycle of abuse, people excuse it by saying things like, "It runs in the family." In other words, "His father has anger issues, so of course he will, too."

That is a dismissive response. It might appear as though you are just supposed to accept how a person behaves, how that person treats you, and how the treatment makes you feel.

To break the cycle of abuse, one must respond instead by saying, "This is where it (the abuse) runs *out* of our family." This might encourage you to speak up, and if necessary, leave the situation to form a healthier lifestyle for your kids to follow.

Being a cycle breaker of generational trauma shows that you are brave. You are powerful.

It can come with a significant cost because some people will try to dismiss, ignore, or talk badly about you. But never underestimate your ability to make a better life for yourself and others.

It is important, sacred work. You do not want to pass the poison to the next generation. Let's give our children a childhood that they don't have to heal from.

Remember: Even if you didn't come from a healthy family, you can still do your best to try to make sure that a healthy family comes from you.

One of my favorite visuals to share with my clients is the anger iceberg. Icebergs are large pieces of ice found floating in the open ocean. What you can see from the surface can be misleading. Most of the iceberg is hidden below the water. Often when we are angry, there are other emotions hidden under the surface, including fear, embarrassment, rejection, helplessness, loneliness, disappointment, worry, and insecurity.

Again, choosing to learn this information about someone DOES NOT excuse their hurtful or abusive words and actions toward you. However, this understanding could assist you with compassion and forgiveness in your healing journey.

Recognizing and Understanding Children's Emotions and Behaviors

> **"Where did we ever get the crazy idea that in order to make children do better, first we have to make them feel worse? Think of the last time you felt humiliated or treated unfairly. Did you feel like cooperating or doing better?"**
> **—Jane Nelson**

The first step in helping your children is understanding their emotions and unmet needs that are driving their behaviors. Children's behaviors could be a direct result from issues at home.

First, keep in mind that often children are punished for being human. Children often are not allowed to have grumpy moods, bad attitudes, disrespectful tones, or bad days. Yet, we adults have them all the time. We must stop holding children to a higher standard than what we can obtain. If we want to see healthier behavior from our children, perhaps we can try setting a healthier example to follow. The story behind a child's behavior can break your heart. And the same for the story behind an adult's behavior.

Here's what a child's emotion might be telling you.

- Mad: Things didn't work out as planned.
- Sad: I'm feeling a loss of some kind.
- Anger: I want to control something I can't.
- Scared: There's something I don't understand.
- Embarrassed: I can see I didn't meet an expectation.

Every day in 100 ways, a child may be asking, "Do you hear me?" Or, "Do you see me?"

When a child can't calm down, they need connection and comfort, not criticism and control.

What Is Emotional Dysregulation?

Do you have a hard time regulating your emotions? Do you wonder what's going on when your emotions feel dysregulated (out of control)? The American Psychological Association (APA) defines dysregulation as "any excessive or otherwise poorly managed mechanism or response." In psychology, a commonly studied type of dysregulation is emotional dysregulation, which has been shown to negatively impact well-being.

Different emotions come and go throughout any given day. Experiencing emotions (even negative ones) is not a problem in and of itself. However, if emotions become overwhelming or out of control, they no longer help us, and they might then actively harm our well-being.

Emotional dysregulation is a complex collection of processes that are thought to include the following four main aspects.

- A lack of awareness, understanding, and acceptance of emotions
- A lack of adaptive strategies for regulating emotions
- An unwillingness to experience emotional distress while pursuing desired goals
- An inability to engage in goal-directed behaviors when experiencing distress

Given these four aspects of emotion dysregulation, here are examples of emotion dysregulation: avoidance, rumination, denial, emotion suppression, aggression, and venting. These mental and behavioral strategies ultimately make negative emotions worse.

The Connection Between Emotions and Needs

A child's or teen's expression of emotions, even challenging ones such as anger or despair, is not inherently problematic. In fact, a developing child relies on the expression of emotion to get their needs met. Crying elicits help for needs an infant cannot meet on their own, such as nourishment or a clean diaper. Coos and giggles encourage a caregiver to continue an activity the child finds rewarding.

For school-age children, emotions provide critical feedback for learning to navigate social relationships, and emotions can either support or undermine the attention and focus necessary for acquiring academic and life skills. For teens—engaged in the developmental process of forming an independent identity—negative emotions can be indicators that boundaries have been crossed, values compromised, or self-care needs (such as sleep) not met.

Skillful emotional regulation relies on several layers of awareness. It involves:

- Being able to identify our own emotions
- Accurately recognizing emotions in others
- Understanding the expectations of our social environment
- Learning how to express or suppress emotions in support of our own goals.

Emotional regulation and child development are supported by a problem-solving mindset: "How can I reinterpret this distressing situation?" Here are some helpful things to offer your child or teenager.

Compassion: Offer compassion, for both yourself and your child. Compassion fosters a sense of connection rather than division. Healthy ways to regulate emotions are a function of the frontal cortex. Already undependable in an immature teenage brain, the frontal cortex goes offline for all of us when we get defensive. The sense of connection fostered by compassion can help keep both you and your child in a rational, problem-solving mindset.

Curiosity: Take a moment to get curious about what unmet need your child's emotion might signal, even if it's coming out sideways. This step can help meet your teen's need to feel heard and understood, which is a universal human need. Curiosity will go a long way toward maintaining a sense of connection with your child and helping them access their capacity for reason, before it goes completely offline if they are overwhelmed by emotion.

Circling back: If emotions—yours or your teen's—overwhelm an interaction, you can revisit the issue. Circle back by naming as many positives about your teen as you can to keep the discussion feeling safe—ideally at least three—before you introduce a different perspective. Building emotional regulation in kids encompasses understanding through experience that emotions are fluid and a rupture in a relationship can be repaired. This will be easier to practice on small ruptures before you try it during bigger blowups.

Creative communication: An intense emotional state can overwhelm a teen's capacity to verbalize their thoughts. Get creative— sometimes it's easier to find a metaphor for a situation than address it directly. ("Where are you on the roller coaster?" "How's the weather for sailing today?") Or perhaps your teen would rather write notes back and forth rather than have a face-to-face conversation. Try to establish a regular routine of checking in, so that it's something that happens on good days as well as bad.

Cognitive skills: Model reflecting on your own emotional life. How do you moderate your own thoughts and behaviors? Describe for your child instances in which you have shifted a negative mindset, seen things from different perspectives, and practiced self-compassion. Your teen may not immediately engage in a similar level of reflection. But more will sink in than they might be willing or able to reveal in the moment.

Understanding Needs

To understand the connection between emotion and needs, you need to first understand what our basic needs are. Abraham Maslow, an American psychologist and philosopher best known for his self-actualization theory of psychology, which argued that the primary goal of psychotherapy should be the integration of the self, stated that people are motivated to achieve certain needs and that some needs take precedence over others.

Our most basic need is for physical survival, and this will be the first thing that motivates our behavior. Once that level is fulfilled, the next level up is what motivates us, and so on. Here is Maslow's hierarchy of needs.

Physiological needs: These are biological requirements for human survival, such as air, food, drink, shelter, clothing, warmth, sex, and sleep. Unless these needs are satisfied, the human body cannot function optimally. Maslow considered physiological needs the most important because all the other needs become secondary until these needs are met.

Safety needs: Once a person's physiological needs are satisfied, the needs for security and safety become salient. People want to experience order, predictability, and control in their lives. These needs include emotional security, financial security, law and order, freedom from fear, social stability, property, health, and wellbeing. These needs can be fulfilled by the family and society (such as the police, schools, businesses, and medical care).

Love and belongingness needs: After physiological and safety needs have been fulfilled, the third level of human needs is social, and it involves feelings of belongingness. Belongingness is an emotional need for interpersonal relationships, affiliating, connectedness, and being part of a group. Examples of belongingness needs include friendship, intimacy, trust, acceptance, receiving and giving affection, and love.

Esteem needs: The fourth level in Maslow's hierarchy, esteem needs include self-worth, accomplishment, and respect. Maslow classified esteem needs into two categories: esteem for oneself (dignity, achievement, mastery, independence) and esteem from others (status, prestige).

Maslow indicated that the need for respect or reputation is most important for children and adolescents and that it precedes real self-esteem or dignity.

Self-actualization needs: These are the highest level in Maslow's hierarchy, and they refer to the realization of a person's potential, self-fulfillment, seeking personal growth and peak experiences. Maslow described this level as the desire to accomplish everything that one can, to become the most that one can be. People perceive or focus on this need very specifically. For example, one person might have a strong desire to become an ideal parent. In another, the desire may be expressed economically, academically, or athletically. For others, it may be expressed creatively, in paintings, pictures, or inventions.

In a violent home, children's needs are often unmet—even the most basic ones. It's easy to understand then that children who have been abused do not have "behavior problems" that need to be addressed. They have extreme survival skills that need to be understood.

When a child is raised by a narcissistic parent, that parent usually is too focused on himself/herself to meet the child's needs. Here are ways that a child raised by a narcissistic (controlling) parent might be affected.

- The child won't feel heard of seen.
- The child's feelings and reality will not be acknowledged.

When trauma and abuse is in your home, you are living in survival mode. This is when you might notice fight, flight, or freeze behaviors in yourself or your children. What does this look or feel like?

When you freeze, you can't move, you don't know what to do, you collapse. You are hurt, and without the proper supports, you might store all those painful emotions away. This can be unprocessed rage, shame, hopelessness.

When you lean toward fight or flight, you are hyper aroused. You might try to be in control or fix the situation. People often want to be able to remove themselves from the trauma in order to heal and build resilience. When you begin to move toward resilience, parts of you start to feel safe to relax, learn, trust, repair, and set boundaries. You learn to self-regulate and find safety. You become compassionate, calm, and confident, and you begin to thrive.

How to Get Support for Your Children

When it comes to treatment for children, I believe a common unfortunate standard is to quickly diagnose and then medicate them. I believe in most cases children would benefit more from therapy in order to discover their unmet needs. The question to ask is, "Are we truly listening when a child is speaking to us?" And perhaps it's not even in their words. Their behaviors might be telling a silent story.

Here are some ways to nurture children's (and adults) mental health.

- Actively listen.
- Be patient.
- Share your feelings.
- Validate their feelings.
- Surround them with healthy adults.
- Teach them how to be safe.
- Ask open-ended questions.
- Model forgiveness.
- Be present.
- Have scheduled family time.

- Respond calmly to their emotions.
- Limits electronics.
- View their behavior as a window into their needs and feelings.
- Hug them if that's comfortable for them.
- Make time to play.
- Set and respect boundaries.
- Teach them to respect your boundaries.
- Recognize positive choices.
- Practice relaxation together.
- Believe in them.
- Be consistent and follow through.
- Model healthy behavior.
- Tell the truth.

I think one of the best things that we can do for our kids is to be transparent: to acknowledge to them that we as adults are also still learning, and we all have room to grow. This frees our kids from expecting perfection from themselves. Perfection is not an achievable goal, and it sets them up for failure.

How to Help

It only takes one person to positively change the course of a child's life. Can that person be you? You don't have to be the child's parent to positively impact their life. How do we advocate for a special child in our life?

Here are a few things to keep in mind that have been helpful for me.

Never stop asking questions. Whether I'm talking with a teacher, doctor, or therapist, I am always asking questions for better understanding and clarification. I ask so many questions that I sometimes feel I should apologize for how many questions I ask. However, asking questions is how we learn. Why would we apologizing for trying to learn?

Never stop expressing you and your child's thoughts/feelings/wants/needs/concerns. Be your child's voice. Even if you don't really understand what is going on yourself, do your best to be present for them, even in their most challenging times. Learn to be calm during their chaos and try to assist them in expressing what they need. Sometimes this could be something basic, such as if they are tired or hungry or other times could be something greater, like they feel unsafe.

Don't be afraid to ask for a second opinion. It is so important that we feel heard. If the support or professional on the other end does not seem to be able to do that, you have the ability to ask for a second opinion. The first answer or guidance you receive might not be the best fit for your child or your family. Even the professionals don't always have the right answers. Research and look for specialists in the area that you or your child are struggling in. I have utilized family therapy services before. There is no shame in admitting that your family needs extra support or guidance to assist you in functioning in a healthier way. School districts can be amazing, and they often have many resources at a family's disposal. Call to find out what your options are.

Educate yourself. I am always reading articles and books to try to understand myself and my children better. A child is not always going to know how to express themselves; they are still learning. A tricky part about parenting is trying to decipher what is going on inside a child's head and body when what we are seeing and hearing doesn't seem to match up to what we are assuming. What we see and hear is not always what is going on. We need to learn how to look under the surface, help them understand and identify what they are feeling, learn how to express their needs and wants, and most importantly learn healthy coping skills. Tell your children that you are going to counseling. Set healthy examples that they don't have to feel ashamed about. Normalize going to counseling, speaking up about feelings and thoughts, learning healthy coping skills, and learning problem solving skills together as a family. Provide a safe

environment for your kids to what to speak to you and learn
with you.

**"There is no such thing as a 'bad kid'—just angry, hurt,
tired, scared, confused, impulsive ones, expressing their
feelings and needs the only way they know how. We owe it
to them to always remember that."
—Dr. Jessica Stephens**

Healing YOUR Inner Child

Have you ever asked yourself, *Why do I keep ending up in the same type of
relationships or surrounded by the same type of people? Why do I keep feeling
like I'm not good enough?*

I still don't truly understand why some people make the choices they
do. I suppose it all comes down to their belief systems.

We get stuck in the "why." We ask ourselves questions like, *Why did
this happen to me? Why did they say or do that?* We desperately want to
understand and make sense of it all so we don't feel crazy. I
encourage you to use "why" in a different way.

Ask yourself, *Why did this happen FOR me?*

Then look for the lesson.

I came across a website called "Becoming the One." After I signed
up, I was sent an inner child meditation. I have passed this along
many times because it can be an emotional and healing activity. I've
adapted it here for you. Record it for yourself, such as on your
phone. Then when you're ready to meditate, find a place that feels
comfortable to lie down with your eyes closed, and if you can, wear
headphones.

*This meditation is for you to connect with your inner child and remember the love
that you are. Begin to notice your breath. Is it shallow? Is it heavy?*

How do you feel? Are you tense or relaxed?

Next notice the sensations in your body. Are any of your muscles tight? Heavy? Achy? Where do you feel that discomfort?

Begin to breathe deeply into any place that you might feel discomfort in your body and let it go. Now begin to relax your body. First, relax your feet. Now relax your thighs. Next relax your belly and your chest. Relax your shoulders and now your jaw. Feel your face relax. Feel everything slowing down as you let your body settle into where you are sitting or lying down.

Now you are going to take a journey to meet your inner child—the little, younger you. Your inner child is innocent, tender, and sensitive.

When we are little, we rely on our parents and caregivers to protect us, nurture us, and give us love. But if our parents were wounded and dealing with their own trauma, they unknowingly hurt us or programmed us with negative beliefs about ourselves.

Now as adults, we are learning to heal and become our own parents and source of divine love. All feelings are welcome here. Your inner child cannot say or do anything wrong in this space. You have full permission to feel whatever comes through.

Now we are going to journey back in time and interact with your inner child. Imagine yourself traveling back into a field of energy and light. Connect with the light that is within you. You are light. You are love. You are born innocent and perfect. Now as you are traveling back, you will find yourself as a small child. Whatever age you travel back to is perfect. Are you three years old? Five years old? Seven years old? Picture yourself as a little child standing in front of you. Take a moment to really notice them. Sit down. Make eye contact.

Ask the younger you if it is okay to hold them in your lap. Take a deep breath and feel the connection with your little child. Now ask them what they are feeling and listen to what they have to say.

Breathe in the understanding that whatever happened to you when you were little, it was not your fault. You were a vulnerable child. It was your caregivers' job to protect you and keep you safe. You have always been worthy of love.

Now speak to your inner child. Let your inner child know that you are loved. You are perfect in every way. I love everything about you.

When we are little, the world can feel like a scary or overwhelming place. It might be that our parents couldn't love us the way we needed them to. Or we felt alone, afraid, or mistreated. Soothe your inner child by saying that you were never responsible for the emotions or actions of other people. It was never your job to take care of other people. It was their job to take care of you, but due to their own pain, they couldn't give you what you needed. And I am so sorry if you every felt unloved or alone.

Now, take a moment to say anything else you want your inner child to hear. Now let your inner child respond and listen to what they have to say for a few moments. Listen intently and if they are quiet, connect with your heart and hold a loving space. Take a moment now to connect.

You are now reconnected to your inner child. This relationship is always here for you. Your inner child will let you know when they are feeling hurt, afraid, angry, sad, or happy. You can let them know that you will listen to their feelings from now on and also that you will make healthy choices to take care of you both.

Before you go, give your inner child a gift to represent the connection you now share, such as a stuffed toy or flower. Visualize the gift you want to give to your inner child and hold it close to your heart. Now, give the gift to your inner child and let them know, I am here for you now. I love you. I'm not going anywhere. You don't have to feel alone again. I will listen to you and take good care of you. This gift is a symbol of our connection, and you are so important to me.

Now, visualize your inner child sitting in your lap. Wrap your arms around them. Feel them wrap their arms around you. Feel your heart connecting to the love you have for your inner child and imagine them becoming translucent and full of light.

Slowly visualize your inner child dissolving into your chest and your heart, merging with your energy so the two of you become one.

Take a deep breathe. And visualize your field full of light. This is the light that has always been in you. You are always worthy. You are good. You have full permission to take care of your heart. You are perfect in every way.

Now, journey back to the present moment. Feel yourself coming back into your space, slowly wiggling your toes and feeling the sensations in your body. Gently stretch your limbs and place your hands on your belly and your heart. Feel the connection that you created with your inner child and remember that they are always there when you want to talk to them or when they want to talk to you. Arrive back in your space full of love, connection, and safety. Take a deep breath and remind your inner child that you are so deeply loved.

Listen to this inner child meditation as often as feels right to you.

Key Concepts to Learn

While you are in the process of understanding and healing your own inner childhood wounds, there are a few key concepts that would be beneficial to learn.

ACEs: On the prevent childhood abuse website, they discuss ACEs (adverse childhood experiences). Their site lists several potential ACEs, such as domestic violence, divorce, emotional neglect, and mental illness. It also shares some adverse community environments, such as discrimination, lack of opportunity, and violence.

The hope is that ACEs are preventable and that people who experience childhood adversity are not guaranteed to negative outcomes in their lives. Positive Childhood Experiences (PCEs) and the Health Outcomes from Positive Experiences (HOPE) framework highlights PCEs in four categories:

- Being in nurturing, supportive relationships
- Living, developing, playing, and learning in safe, stable, protective, and equitable environments
- Having opportunities for constructive social engagement and connectedness
- Leaning social and emotional competencies

This work can help build our collective understanding of preventing ACEs and building resilience. Central to child adversity prevention is creating safe, stable, nurturing relationships and environments for all children and families.

You can go online to take a test to identify your ACEs score.

Have you ever wondered why you seem to end up in the same type of relationships over and over again? It's important to understand how we attach to others and where those attachments stem from. Here are the attachment styles.

Secure attachment: This attachment style signifies a warm, loving bond between parent and child. The child feels loved and cared for and develops the ability to form healthy relationships with people around them. Children with secure attachment styles are active and demonstrate confidence in their interactions with others.

People who develop secure attachment styles in childhood are likely to carry this healthy way of bonding into adulthood. They generally have no problem building long-term relationships without fear of abandonment.

Anxious-ambivalent attachment: Anxious-ambivalent children tend to distrust caregivers, and this insecurity often means that their environment is explored with trepidation rather than excitement. They constantly seek approval from their caregivers and continuously observe their surroundings for fear of being abandoned.

People who developed under the anxious-ambivalent attachment style tend to carry what they have learned into adulthood. They very often feel unloved by their partners and find it difficult to express love and connection. People who developed attachments under this style are usually emotionally dependent in adulthood.

Avoidant attachment: Children who have developed under the avoidant style have learned to accept that their emotional needs are likely to remain unmet and continue to grow up feeling unloved and insignificant. They often struggle with expressing their feelings and find it hard to understand emotions. In adulthood, they tend to avoid intimate relationships.

Disorganized attachment: This is a combination of avoidant and anxious attachment, and children who fit into this group often display intense anger and rage. They may break toys and behave in other volatile ways. They also have difficult relationships with caregivers.

Children developed under the disorganized attachment style tend to avoid intimate relationships as adults. They can very easily explode and have a difficult time controlling their emotions.

Trauma often leads to a disoriented-disorganized attachment. A disorganized attachment pattern in turn imparts an increased risk of further abuse and neglect.

Where is the proof of trauma when it isn't physical abuse? Our body keeps the score. A book by Bessel van der Kolk, *The Body Keeps the Score*, is an inspiring story of how a group of therapists and scientists—together with their courageous, memorable patients—struggled to integrate recent advances in brain science, attachment research, and body awareness into treatments that can free trauma survivors from the tyranny of the past. These new paths to recovery activate the brain's natural neuroplasticity to rewire disturbed functioning and rebuild step by step the ability to "know what you know and feel what you feel." They also offer experiences that directly counteract the helplessness and invisibility associated with trauma, enabling both adults and children to reclaim ownership of their bodies and their lives.

Drawing on more than 30 years at the forefront of research and clinical practice, Bessel van der Kolk shows that the terror and isolation at the core of trauma literally reshape both brain and body. New insights into our survival instincts explain why traumatized people experience incomprehensible anxiety and numbing and intolerable rage, and how trauma affects their capacity to concentrate, remember, form trusting relationships, and even feel at home in their own bodies. Having lost the sense of control of themselves and frustrated by failed therapies, they often fear that they are damaged beyond repair.

For example, you might notice your jaw becoming clenched or you might feel the knots forming in your back and shoulders. PTSD can show up in the body. The trauma isn't our fault, but the healing is our responsibility. We deserve to live as the healthiest version of ourselves.

I love to read, and for me one step more enjoyable than reading is completing a workbook. Anything that encourages us to dig deeper and learn more about ourselves—the way we think, feel, act—in my opinion, is time well spent. Even as you are healing, your body still might hold onto the trauma. If you choose to do a workbook, here are some ideas to keep in mind.

- Trauma alters our ability to think. It causes severe damage that can only be reversed when the body acknowledges that the danger is no longer there.
- The effect of trauma on people can be deep-seated; it haunts the victim even long after the traumatic incident.
- Wealth, accolades, and accomplishments cannot obliterate trauma.
- Sometimes, traumatized people will instinctively recreate the toxic experiences, hoping to master a painful situation and resolve it for good. However, repeating the experience merely aggravates the pain.
- Although drugs and medication enable people to function from day to day, core issues are not adequately addressed, so people are unable to regain complete control of their lives
- It takes longer for a traumatized person's level of stress hormones to return to normal, which makes them prone to irritability, lack of attention, long-term health issues, memory problems, and sleep disorders.
- In the face of danger, we respond in three ways: fight, flight, or freeze.
- Each trauma victim responds differently to the same experience.
- Some trauma survivors get stuck in the past and find it challenging to live in the present. They react to situations at times irrationally, alienating from others, and shame

becomes the main emotion that leaves them preoccupied with hiding the truth.

- Intense negative emotions affect both the heart and the gut.
- Many traumatized individuals have defense systems that are too strong that they fail to enjoy life.
- Research shows that continued exposure to emotional abuse and neglect is as shattering as being a victim of physical and sexual abuse.
- There must be emotional attunement between the child and the caregiver to create a haven for the child.
- The first caregivers in our lives influence our perception of reality and how we connect with others. They feed our brain with information that forms our inner maps.
- Traumatized children share three characteristics: a persistent dysregulation pattern, attention and concentration problems, and attunement difficulty with self and others.
- The quality of a parent's interaction with a child can determine the child's behavior in life.
- Ordinary memory is social and involves telling a story for a purpose. The traumatic memory is a reenactment of experiences that are alienating and humiliating. It can be lonely and unchanging.
- Trauma is devastating, unbelievable, and agonizing. Nobody wants to remember it.
- Nobody can undo a traumatic experience, but you can address its impressions on the mind, body, and soul.
- Trauma strips you of the feeling of being in control of yourself, and you can recover to reestablish ownership of yourself, to freely feel and know what you feel without shame, anger, or discomfort.
- Recovery from trauma can happen when the memories of the traumatic experiences are integrated into your life, when the memories no longer dominate you and your life feels meaningful.
- Therapists believe in the power of talk to address trauma.

Keeping silent about it can make a victim feel isolated. Acknowledging and putting a label to the experience and being listened to can be liberating to a trauma survivor and remove them from feelings of fear, anger, terror, and shame. Sometimes a victim can only accept the truth after repeatedly telling their story.

- A good support network is a powerful safeguard against trauma.
- A lot of psychiatric problems started as an adaptive strategy for self-protection.
- Talk therapy may be effective if the emotional brain does not overpower the rational brain.
- Healing from trauma can only take place when the "victim" learns to accept the reality.

There are four fundamental truths to consider when trying to heal:

1. Healthy relationships breed healthy well-being.
2. Communication allows us to change ourselves, influence others, and share a common purpose with them.
3. We can control how our body and brain function.
4. We can help create a safe environment for both children and adults.

When we recognize and apply these truths, we can help people heal from trauma and empower them to regain their self-esteem. Encourage a trauma victim to participate in decision making to make them feel they still have control over some parts of their lives. If the trauma victim is a child, you might ask them to decide on simple things such as choose how to spend the weekend or what they want for dinner. Be sure to surround yourself with people who can help you achieve your goal of healing.

Digging Deeper

Now that you have reconnected with the little, younger you, you might realize that you have to digger deeper to understand your unresolved wounds. If you want something that you never had, such as a healthier version of you or a healthier life, you might have to do something that you've never done, such as dig deep or ask for help.

Take the time to identify which of your needs were not met in your childhood and/or other relationships. This main be painful to navigate.

Consider forgiving your parents. They, too, might have had childhoods that they didn't heal from. Possibly they didn't know what they were doing to you because they never experienced unconditional love themselves. You won't be able to change them, but this provides you with the opportunity to heal and break the cycle.

We can learn how to reparent ourselves. We can learn how to love ourselves unconditionally the way we always deserved. We can learn how to meet our own needs, instead of depending on others to meet our needs.

We can choose to blame our parents or other people in our lives for our pain, but once you are old enough to put your hands on the wheel and steer yourself in a new direction, please choose the path of healing.

You might also need to forgive yourself. Forgive yourself for not knowing better at the time. Forgive yourself for giving your power away. Forgive yourself for your past behaviors, patterns, and traits that you picked up while dealing with trauma. Forgive yourself for who you were while you were trying to survive.

Feeling Your Feelings

We typically don't want to feel pain, sadness, anger, or any emotions other than happiness or joy. Unfortunately, those "gross" emotions are part of the healing journey.

I understand that when we step out of our homes every morning, most of us probably put on some sort of mask—a mask that hides our childhood wounds, our marital issues, our low self-esteem. We hold our breath, hoping that we make it through the day without someone detecting our vulnerability. We are scared to let people in. I think the reason why is that we created our own problems the moment that we were show how to shame, judge, and criticize.

When someone asks, "How are you?" do they really want to know? Or do they just want a smile, nod, and "I'm good" response? Let's keep things moving along. We don't have time to actually care about others or ourselves.

Do you ever look at our world and wonder, *How did our world become so unhealthy?*

Now how do we collectively come together to fix it and make it healthier?

I believe we are often surrounded by divide. I think many of us have forgotten that we are all fighting for the same team: humanity.

Circling back around to you: If you take the time to heal yourself, you will add something healthier into the lives of other people. It's a domino effect.

And if you have identified a cycle, a pattern of abuse in your life, how do you break that cycle of abuse? You could break it by leaving.

Even after using all your strength to decide to leave, you need more strength.

Please keep in mind specialists in that area can guide you through that. The most important thing to keep in mind is: Are you doing your best to keep yourself healthy? The only thing you can control is the interactions that you are choosing to have with your children.

Be careful what you tolerate. You are teaching other people how to treat you.

~

Nicole's Story

What was the most difficult part of being in a domestic violence relationship?

The most difficult part for me was not even knowing I *was* in a domestic violence relationship until years later. He destroyed my personhood, making me think I was crazy. Not being able to have a say, speak my mind, or have an opinion. Losing my identity. Having to watch what I said, when I said it, and how I said it. Being treated more like a daughter than a wife. He belittled me and called me names like idiot, stupid, moron, useless. He told me without him I am nothing. He made me feel incompetent and worthless. Having my kids witness this type of behavior toward their mother and thinking this was normal to treat women this way is what really pushed me to get out of this toxic relationship.

What was the most difficult part about leaving a domestic violence relationship?

I was afraid to leave because of how bad my mind had been manipulated into thinking I was nothing without my husband. He made me quit my job to be a stay-at-home mom, and he controlled all our finances, making it extremely difficult for me to leave, not knowing how I would support myself and two young boys. Fear of the unknown. Leaving everything that I had known: the life that I knew, the routine. Doubting myself made it extremely hard to leave. It was also hard to leave because he never physically harmed me, so I thought, *It's not too bad here. Maybe he will change.* We had seen numerous counselors over the years, and once we'd complete our sessions, he would go back to being somewhat normal and kind.

It's like a vicious cycle. Sometimes I almost felt as if he was bipolar, not knowing what to expect or when to expect it.

What guidance would you give to someone else who is trying to leave or trying to heal after leaving?

Go with your gut instinct. Be truthful with yourself. Find a good support system—family, friends, or a good church. Have an exit strategy. I educated myself on domestic violence and what it looks like, and that was extremely helpful and healing for me. Also plug into support groups to help you along with the whole process. Once you have the knowledge and the right words to describe what it is that you've been going through and feeling, you will realize you're not crazy and the relationship indeed is toxic.

A Word about Not Taking Sides

Rather than taking sides, acknowledge that all parties involved in abusive situations need help. Maybe the abuser doesn't recognize that they have the ability to make positive change for themselves and everyone around them. It's possible that the abusers are the ones who need more help than the victims because the "abusive mentality " leads them to believe that it's okay to hurt people and lie about it, and it's okay to hurt someone just make sure you keep it hidden. If these individuals are not held accountable, they continue to live with this belief system and potentially continue to hurt others. Speaking up is how you can potentially get it to stop.

Let It Go

I think that we often make a mistake by assuming when we tell people to just "let go" that somehow that is easy to accomplish. That couldn't be further from the truth. I think saying "just let go" might even be a way to dismiss someone. "Just let it go already."

Depending on what someone has been through, especially something traumatic, letting go is not part of the solution. Talking, processing, feeling, and healing are how we reach a point of letting go. I think it's crucial to understand this concept.

This is what I think about when I read the poem "She Let Go" by Reverend Safire Rose. That poem has crossed my path in several different areas over the past few years. I don't think that's a coincidence. Sometimes during a messy healing journey, you reach the point of "letting go" when you least expect it. You can read the poem at https://safire-rose.com/books-and-media/poetry/she-let-go

"Never underestimate a cycle breaker. Not only did they experience years of generational trauma, but they stood in the face of that trauma and fought to say, 'This ends with me.' This is brave. This is powerful. This comes at a significant cost."
—Nate Postlethwait

FOUR

MY JOURNEY

***If someone tells you 'You can't,' they are showing you
their limits, not yours.***

As a child, my role in my family was the "fixer." I think that I
assumed that role because helping others met my need to feel
worthy.

Being in that role as a child ultimately led me to the career of being
a licensed therapist. Because of that, I want to be grateful that was
the role I filled.

Although overall I appreciate that I define myself as a helper, I
acknowledge that the other side of that coin was becoming a people
pleaser. I believe the main challenge of a people pleasing mentality
is that your own wants and needs often get put on the back burner.

We see in ourselves what we want to see. For many years, I viewed
these traits as healthy. I'm a firm believer that we continue to be put
in similar situations until we learn the necessary lesson. So, I
remember several times in my life when I became completely
drained by consistently trying to make other people in my life
happy.

When you go through a challenging healing journey, you realize that your own happiness truly matters.

One visualization that has always been beneficial for me was to think of a butterfly coming out of a cocoon. You have to be in a moment of darkness before you can shed your old self and emerge as the new, healthier you! It was learning to let go of my people-pleasing, fixer role that set me free to focus on my own healing journey. Here are some helpful things to remember:

I can:

- Cut you off AND still love you.
- Stop speaking to you AND still care about you.
- Let you go AND still wish you the best.

I think we live in a world where we are prone to give a diagnosis and prescribe medication. Both professionally and personally, I don't think that's the healthiest solution. I understand medication can be essential at times, but I don't think it should be the only treatment in most cases. The led me to looking for a community of resources who specialized in holistic modalities. I had the pleasure of meeting Reverend Lyn S. Felix, LCSW, CHT, RM, who educated me on the following healing options.

~

Expert Q&A: Reverend Lyn S. Felix, LCSW, CHT, RM

Reverend Lyn S. Felix, LCSW, CHT, RM, is a holistic and integrative psychotherapist and hypnotherapist serving individuals from school age through adult, couples, and families. Lyn's empathy, compassion, and interpersonal skills help clients feel safe, secure, and understood as they process their feelings, thoughts, and life concerns.

Lyn brings her intuitive gifts and years of field experience into her counseling, coaching, and ministering practice. Clients overcome long held, limiting beliefs and habits, freeing themselves to access their potential more fully. Clients can also safely access hidden or stuck core emotions, feelings, and memories and release distress and trauma. This allows past experiences to be healed and integrated into the past life story and no longer create daily overwhelm or overreacting.

Using her extensive knowledge of mindfulness, energy psychology, Reiki, and breathing practices, Lyn teaches effective, mind-body toolbox skills for being present, grounded, calm, resilient, and hopeful.

What do you feel are some of the best holistic modalities that someone can learn about and participate in to feel relief from trauma and to heal?

- **Energy psychology EFT (Tapping)** is acupuncture without needles. It's based on Traditional Chinese Medicine. Each organ of the body has an energy flow path, and there are locations where you can access the organs. When a person is in balance, the life force energy flows smoothly. When in distress, the life force energy may be stuck or leaking. By gently tapping with soft part of fingers on specific sequence of points (acupressure) the head, body, hands, while saying feeling words that match the distress, the strength of what bothers a person is reduced and more positive feelings can be felt.
- **Energy medicine,** such as Donna Eden's protocols through Inner Source, teaches a multitude of practices, in simple movements that can release, anxiety, anger, overwhelm, and much more. Practices moving hands over the head "Crown Pull" or breathing and circling the body to release anger "Expelling the venom" or gently tapping on the sternum are effective practices. Besides learning from a therapist, a client can watch many videos online for regular practice.
- **Breathing practices** include much more than breathing deeply. Alternate nostril breathing, unilateral breathing, continuous breathing, and square breathing are some popular ways to calm and recenter. Many breathing

practices can activate the vagus nerve and bring relief and calm.

- **Mindfulness based stress reduction** is a wonderful way to practice being present and coming into the body. Such examples as mindful walking, mindful eating, mindful gazing, and listening to guided meditations serve as ways to center, ground, and focus calmly on what is happening in this moment. This reduces the monkey mind of constant mind chatter, and it might even dissolve the chatter.

- **Focusing,** a practice developed by Eugene Gendlin, has a variety of ways to encourage and support a person's attention inward. My favorite has been inter-relational focusing with a partner. One person is companion, the other focuses. Companion provides support to assist the focuser to go more deeply within. Many insights can be revealed from this.

- **Brainspotting** is an elegant way for a person working with a therapist to connect to the deep part within their brain, where core healing can take place. Where we look with our eyes is connected to how we feel. A form of focused mindfulness, Brainspotting can benefit the deactivation of distress, trauma, and habits. Brainspotting can also be used to enhance growth and expansive potential.

- **Hypnosis** is a trance state, where the activity of the brain slows down from waking state beta to alpha, theta, or delta. All people can learn self-hypnosis and use it to relax and reach their life goals. Clinical hypnotherapy is helpful in releasing and untangling the strength of painful memories and fears. Using relaxing trance state enables a person to safely go back in time to dissolve trauma and pain and also to go forward in the future to enhance feelings of confidence, safety, and peace.

- **Spiritual and intuitive counseling** recognizes and connects God, Divine, Guardians, Guides, and Angels in the most comforting way for the client. Through inquiry, prayers, and shared intention, healing and insights are revealed.

- **Vibrational sound therapy** can be experienced through playing seven metal singing bowls, crystal bowls, gongs, or using voice to soothe and relax the nervous system.
- **Biofield tuning** is a relaxing, rejuvenating experience from a trained practitioner. The person is fully clothed and can be lying on a massage table or sitting on a chair. Treatment is given using weighted tuning forks gently touching the body to access and rebalance the body's life force into a healthy flow. Unweighted tuning forks are used in the field all around the person to clear static from distress or trauma that has affected the person over time. Tuning forks applied in this way shift our energetic frequency to more coherence, calm, and clarity.

If someone is unable to afford these services, what are some free healthy skills that one can use on their own?

Nature is a great healing resource. Consider walking, bicycling, gardening, and even lying on a blanket and gazing up at the clouds. Being near water, such as a pond, river, stream, or the ocean, is helpful. While lying on the floor, alternate lifting arm and leg as high as comfortable. Singing, humming, and listening to music are beneficial. Dancing is a great practice. Self-massage, showering, and yoga stretching can release a lot of body tension.

What other main points would be important to know about using holistic modalities to heal from trauma?

I have found having an internal readiness capacity for change impacts a person's ability to benefit from holistic modalities. If the person's nervous system and thoughts are activated and in overwhelm, it may not be the best time for the person to be shown holistic practices. And in this case, the person may feel more distress that they cannot concentrate or receive the help. For example, consider the importance of connecting to breathing and allowing the breath to be as it is, before offering a suggestion on how to breathe.

The holistic therapist needs to be extremely sensitive and present to the person's state of being. Speaking in a calming voice and attuning to the person's responses, with gently inquiry, the therapist will sense how or what simple grounding practices to offer. It is crucial for the therapist and the environment to feel safe, non-triggering, and comfortable for the client.

During your healing, you need to offer yourself love, kindness, compassion, and understanding. It's a battle of learning what to hold onto tighter and what to let go of. Holding on tight might mean that you are trying to be in control because you are afraid. You might fear that if you let go, things will all fall apart and things could end up worse than they already are. You want to feel heard, seen, understood, loved. You want help. Are you breaking your own heart by trying to stay somewhere that you clearly don't belong? As difficult as it is, it can be beneficial and healthy to learn how to let some people go.

The following poem by Anthony Hopkins is an excellent example of writing that supported me on my healing journey.

Let Go of People Who Are Not Prepared to Love You

Let go of people who are not prepared to love you.

This is the hardest thing you will have to do in your life.

And it will also be the most important thing.

Stop having hard conversations with people who don't want change.

Stop showing up for people who have no interest in your presence.

I know your instinct is to do everything to earn the appreciation of those around you.

But it's a boost that steals your time, energy, mental and physical health.

When you begin to fight for a life with joy, interest, and commitment, not everyone will be ready to follow you in this place.

This doesn't mean you need to change what you are.

It means you should let go of the people who aren't ready to accompany you.

If you are excluded, insulted, forgotten, or ignored by the people you give your time to…

…you don't do yourself a favor by continuing to offer your energy and your life.

The truth is…

You are not for everyone.

And not everyone is for you.

That's what makes it so special when you meet people who reciprocate love.

You will know how precious you are.

The more time you spend trying to make yourself loved by someone who is unable to, the more time you waste depriving yourself of the possibility of this connection to someone else.

There are billions of people on this planet.

And many of them will meet with you at your level of interest and commitment.

The more you stay involved with people who use you as a pillow, a background option, or a therapist for emotional healing, the longer you stay away from the community you want.

Maybe if you stop showing up, you won't be wanted.

And maybe if you stop trying, the relationship will end.

Or maybe if you stop texting, your phone will stay dark for weeks.

That doesn't mean you ruined the relationship. It means the only thing holding it back was the energy that only you gave to keep it.

This is not love.

It's attachment.

It's wanting to give a chance to those who don't deserve it.

You deserve so much.

There are people who should not be in your life.

The most valuable things you have in your life is your time and energy.

Both are limited.

When you give your time and energy, it will define your existence.

And when you realize this…

You begin to understand why you are so anxious when you spend time with people, in activities, places, or situations that don't suit you and shouldn't be around you, your energy is stolen.

You will begin to realize that the most important thing you can do for yourself (and for everyone around you) is to protect your energy more fiercely than anything else.

Make your life a safe haven, in which only "compatible "people are allowed.

You're not responsible for saving anyone.

You are not responsible for convincing them to improve. It's not your work to exist for people and give your life to them!

If you feel bad, if you feel compelled, you will be the root of all your problems, fearing that they will not return the favors you have granted.

It's your only obligation to realize that you are the love of your destiny.

And accept the love you deserve.

Decide that you deserve true friendship, commitment, true and complete love with healthy and prosperous people.

Then wait and see how much everything begins to change.

Don't waste time with people who are not worth it. Change will give you the love, esteem, happiness, and protection you deserve.

Let go of the person who broke your heart.

—Anthony Hopkins

My Playlist

One of the most difficult parts of healing is being able to get out of your own head. A technique I've found helpful is listening to music. I believe that music is a universal healing tool.

No matter how you're feeling—happy, sad, confused—chances are you can find a song with lyrics that can support your mood. Despite what's going on around you, you can take a mindful moment—or three to five minutes—and lose yourself in your favorite song.

Be your true self in this moment. If that means roll down your car windows, crank up the music, and sing at the top of your lungs, do it!

Don't be afraid to include your kids on your musical adventures.

Here's my personal playlist. What's yours?

Inspirational Strength-Building Songs

- "Fight Song" by Rachel Platten
- "Fearless" by Jasmine Murray
- "Speechless" by Naomi Scott
- "I'm Still Standing" by Elton John
- "Survivor" by Destiny's Child
- "Through the Rain" by Mariah Carey
- "I Hope You Dance" by Lee Ann Womack
- "Set It All Free" by Scarlett Johansson

- "Firework" by Katy Perry
- "Hold My Hand" by Jess Glynne
- "Stand by you" by Rachel Platten
- "The Climb" by Miley Cyrus
- "My Wish" by Rascal Flatts
- "Count on Me" by Bruno Mars
- "Lean on Me" by Bill Withers
- "I'm Standing with You" by Chrissy Metz

Spiritual Songs

- "Lord, I Need You" by Matt Maher
- "In Jesus Name" by Katy Nichole
- "This Little Light of Mine" by Addison Road
- "How Could Anyone" by Shaina Noll
- "You Keep Hope Alive" by Mandisa
- "Battle Belongs" by Phil Wickman
- "10,000 Reasons" by Matt Redman
- "Way Maker" by Leeland
- "Anthem" by Phil Wickman
- "Even If" by Mercyme
- "Death Was Arrested" by North Point Worship
- "Magnify" by We Are Messengers
- "How He Loves Us" by David Crowder Band
- "After all (holy)" by David Crowder Band
- "Multiplied" by Need to Breathe
- "I Lift My Hands" by Chris Tomlin
- "Hold on to Me" by Lauren Daigle
- "Back to You" by Mandisa
- "The Prayer" by Celine Dion and Josh Groban
- "You Raise Me Up" by Josh Groban

Children's Song:

- "Shine Your Way" by Owl City
- "How Far I'll Go" by Auli'I Cravalho (*Moana*)

- "A Whole New World" by Lea Salonga, Brad Kane (*Aladdin*)
- "Try Everything" by Shakira (*Zootopia*)
- "You and Me" by Dove Cameron (*Descendants 2*)
- "Hooray! We Did It" (*Dora the Explorer*)
- "Together We Stand" by Ariana Greenblatt (*Boss Baby 2*)
- "Keep the Beat" by Lin-Manuel Miranda (*Vivo*)
- "Good Mood" by Adam Levine (*Paw Patrol*)
- "So Much World" by Anya Taylor-Joy (*Playmobil*)
- "It's Gonna Be a Lovely Day" by Lunchmoney Lewis (*Pets 2*)

Move-Your-Body Song: "Better When I'm Dancin'" by Meghan Trainor

Studies show moving your body can get you out of a traumatic flashback state.

Stories and anecdotes can help also, such as the following Tale of the Two Wolves.

The Tale of the Two Wolves

This Native American story features two characters: a grandfather and his grandson. The grandfather explains to his grandson that there are two wolves fighting within him, which is an image that serves as a metaphor for the man's inner sense of conflict. The conversation between the two men goes like this:

"I have a fight going on in me," the old man said. "It's taking place between two wolves. One is evil. He is anger, envy, sorrow, regret, greed, arrogance, self-pity, guilt, resentment, inferiority, lies, false pride, superiority, and ego. The other embodies positive emotions. He is joy, peace, love, hope, serenity, humility, kindness, benevolence, empathy, generosity, truth, compassion, and faith. Both wolves are fighting to the death."

The same fight is going on inside you and every other person, too."

The grandson looked up at his grandfather and asked, "Which wolf will win?"

The old Cherokee gave a simple reply. "The one you feed."

This parable serves as a powerful reminder of the fight that every human being must face. Regardless of the type of person you are or what kind of life you lead, you will find yourself battling two conflicting emotions at some point in your life. Whether the fight is between anger and peace or resentment and compassion, it's important to recognize the conflicting feelings inside you and to feed the values and choices that matter most.

When you show up authentic, you create the space for others to do the same.

FIVE

FAITH-BASED TRAUMA HEALING

"Faith as small as a mustard seed can move mountains."
—Matthew 17:20

Have you ever felt lost? Whether you consider yourself a spiritual person or not, there might have been a time in your life when you were looking for a sign or guidance, wanting a higher power to show you the way.

This isn't just about spirituality. Do you have a secure, loving, accepting group of people who make you feel heard and build you up? Finding a group that you connect with and be vulnerable around can help. As we grow up, we might recognize that the church, family, or groups that we were associated with don't necessarily align with us anymore. Doing what's right for you can come with a lot of hardships.

I feel like I've spent years trying to develop the spiritual side of myself. It wasn't until the toughest moments of my life that my spirituality strengthened.

I realized that although someone's spiritual journey could be done alone, my preference was to have a group of people who aligned with my path. That is when I came across the Gate Community Church, in Bethlehem, Pennsylvania, and its pastor, Eric Schwartz.

What led me to that environment was the realness that I felt from those around me: vulnerability, honesty, tears, trauma, hardship. We're not faking it or wearing masks in front of each other. We show our real selves, wounds and all.

My church introduced me to a program called Faith-Based Trauma Healing.

The therapist in me was jumping for joy, which probably sounds silly, because now I had the opportunity to combine two of my passions: therapy and spirituality. This was probably the first time in years that I chose to work on healing myself—instead of healing others. We've all heard the metaphor of putting your own oxygen mask on before helping others. I so desperately wanted to breathe.

I think we underestimate the power of connection. You take that first scary step, walking out of your home, away from that relationship. The next scary step might be going into a support group or church. Then next year, you could be in a healthier place because you took that one scary step that led you to a healthier, happier life.

~

Expert Q&A: Pastor Eric Schwartz

Eric Schwartz is pastor of The Gate Community Church in Bethlehem, Pennsylvania, and a podcaster for Evancynical, a biweekly podcast where Eric dives deep in to the stories of people who have been let down, disappointed, abused, and traumatized by the Evangelical church, where they are today in their spiritual journey, and where they are finding hope.

What is The Gate Community Church's mission?

We are an intentionally small church. I've been a part of and visited mega churches where the focus of the ministry is the Sunday morning gathering. In and of itself, that is not entirely negative, but there can be a lack of connection and intimacy between the pastor and the congregation. When we look at Jesus, his style of disciple-ship (churchy word for mentoring) was very intimate and relational. The current model of church lacks this method of pastoring. What we are seeing is essentially a weekly Ted Talk.

At The Gate Community Church, we strive to tear down that paradigm by avoiding the Ted Talk model and engaging in an authentic, vulnerable, and conversational model of preaching. This allows the parishioners to actively engage with the content and topic. This creates a safe place for questioning and doubt, which is essential to spiritual growth. I often learn so much myself listening to the perspectives of those I'm teaching.

What are your goals?

Our hope is that we are creating a safe place where not only am I being vulnerable about my doubts and struggles, but also those in the congregation. This helps people to know they are not alone. We all struggle. We all doubt. We are all in pain. And we all get through it.

In his New Testament letter Galatians, St. Paul mandated his readers and listeners to carry each other's burdens (Galatians 6:2). When we share our struggles publicly, this is what we are asking of those in our church community.

When we speak up about mental health and trauma, we are removing the stigma and shame. The church should be a place of healing. Hopefully by creating a safe space to share, we can help people heal.

What resources do you recommend?

Some resources we often mention and offer is the American Bible Society's Trauma Healing Initiative, https://ministry.american-bible.org/trauma-healing. And of course, counseling and spiritual direction.

Expert Q&A Kathy Emeigh

Kathy Emeigh was introduced to Spiritual Mirroring in July 2017 via Richard Rohr's book "Falling Upward." She began her formal spiritual direction work in 2019 and completed her certification in 2021 through Oasis Ministries. Kathy resides in the Lehigh Valley, Pennsylvania, with her husband, Paul, and her dog, Oliver John. Her four married adult children, their spouses, and her eight adorable grandchildren all live in the Lehigh Valley, too.

What is "spiritual direction?"

It's also known as spiritual companioning, mirroring, guiding. Perhaps you are someone who desires deeper relationships, with God, with yourself, and with others.

This kind of spiritual journey by its very nature longs to be explored in the company of another. Jesus said, "For where two or three are gathered in My name; I am there in the midst of them." (Matthew 18:20 NKJV). Spiritual direction creates a space where two gather to focus on an awareness of God in their midst.

Imagine yourself and a companion in a conversation where the Spirit of God joins you.

Imagine a conversation where you are held in the "Vast Love of God."

Spiritual direction is a path that cultivates this kind of companioning, authenticity, renewal, transformation, and healing.

Spiritual direction is an ancient spiritual practice vitally relevant today. If you have a deep desire to know God better or wish to have a fellow traveler with whom you can talk to and ponder the Spirit's presence and leading in their life, then you may be yearning for the practice of Spiritual direction.

Spiritual direction provides a spiritual "mirror" for you as well as space where you are listened to and held in God's presence. The director is trained to actively listen to you as well as to the Spirit of God. They are trained to watch, with the seeker for the Divine

Movement of God; the director may "mirror" your words back to you, asking you questions that only you can answer.

For example: Where is God in this moment? What is God up to in this? How is God loving you here? What are you feeling invited to in this?

It's about opening the moment to God. Any moment will do. Every story, experience, and dynamic, is a way into the moment and consequently, a way into God.

In essence, the spiritual director and you are fellow sojourners, purposefully journeying life with one another to grow deeper in an authentic relationship with God. As you deepen in your God-relationship, you will also ultimately and positively affect your relationships with yourselves and with others.

Spiritual direction is a safe, confidential place offering strong support to help traverse your life journeys. Sessions are usually once a month and last approximately one hour. The directee determines how frequently they wish to meet.

Spiritual direction is not considered counseling. Counseling tends to be crisis-oriented or problem-driven, aiming to solve particular problems or handle specific crises. That is not the goal of spiritual direction. The spiritual direction relationship takes the long view. It looks at how God is working, calling, prodding, and inviting us to new ways of being with the Divine in the midst of our lives.

"Spiritual direction provides an "address" on the house of your life so that you can be "addressed" by God in prayer. When this happens, your life begins to be transformed in ways you hadn't planned or counted on, for God works in wonderful and surprising ways."
—Henri Nouwen, Spiritual Direction: Wisdom for the Long Walk of Faith

I love the beauty of connection, and I feel blessed to have been aligned with many through my healing journey. The Gate Community Church and pastor Eric led me to Jane Consiglio LPC, who is certified as a facilitator for faith-based trauma healing and introduced me to it.

This is where I first heard the term "heart wound." A heart wound can be invisible, but it shows up in the person's behavior. It can be painful and must be treated with care. If ignored, it is likely to get worse. The pain has to be expressed. If people pretend their emotional wounds are healed when really they are not, it will often cause them greater problems. Heart wounds can attract bad things if not healed. It takes time to heal a heart wound. People can experience healing, some believe from God, from others, from medicine, etc. The individual is never the same version of themselves before the heart wound occurred. A heart wound can cause intense fear, helplessness, hopelessness, and a sense of grief and loss.

The healing through faith-based group includes working through the process of suffering, being heard, grieving, lamenting, bringing pain to the cross, forgiving, rebuilding, and developing resilience.

When our hearts are wounded, it greatly affects our lives. We may behave in three ways: reliving the experience, avoiding reminders of the trauma, and being on alert all the time. The wounds of the heart can become more serious when they cause us to feel shamed and a sense that we are bad or flawed, something that forces us to act in a way that goes against our beliefs, or something that goes on for a long time.

The moment that we step into an environment or group that acknowledges that trauma exists and validates our pain, we can begin healing. What happens when we talk about our pain? We gain an honest understanding of what happened and how it has affected us. We express our feelings about what happened. We try to accept what happened. We should feel heard and know that we are not alone.

The trauma and grief journey can go hand in hand. It may begin with a crisis or loss. It can take you through denial, anger, and hopelessness. With hard work, you will arrive at new beginnings.

Denial allows us to absorb the loss little by little and keeps us from feeling overwhelmed. Anger can be a way of fighting against the loss when we feel helpless. We can feel numb, lonely, or guilty. While we are going through that beautiful mess of healing, it's crucial that we are choosing to surround ourselves with good listeners.

Who is a good listener? A good listener creates a safe space. They show that they care about you. They allow you to talk without interruption. They do not force you to share more than you are comfortable sharing. They do not criticize you, preach to you, nor try to give you quick solutions. They do not minimize your pain by comparing it to their own.

Here are three helpful questions that a good listener might ask.

- What happened?
- How do you feel?
- What was the hardest part for you?

A good listener will allow you to speak at your own pace. A good listener will respect your healing process. They will notice when you are distressed. They may encourage you to pause or take a deep breath. They may pray for you or with you. They try to listen, validate, and understand your pain. They keep information confidential.

The emotional release we feel in a safe environment is necessary for healing, growth, and renewal. We learn how to forgive ourselves and others. We learn to surrender what we can't control. Forgiveness and surrender, which both can be challenging to learn and implement, also have the ability to provide us with freedom. Also acknowledging that even if an individual is able to surrender and forgive, it does not mean that reconciliation is the next step, not in the cases of domestic violence and abuse. It does not require for us to trust the person again. Forgiveness is an ongoing process of reaffirming our decision to let go each time we remember the pain. Whether faith is part of your healing journey or not, we should all be allowed to be authentic and vulnerable and speak the truth of our hearts.

~

Expert Q&A: Jane Consiglio LPC

Jane M. Consiglio, RN, LPC, is a licensed counselor and the Trauma Healing Ministry Manager at Cornerstone Counseling Ministries in Easton, Pennsylvania. Through the Trauma Healing Institute's Healing the Wounds of Trauma program, she has been certified as a Master Facilitator. Her passion is to serve women who have been victims of human trafficking and domestic violence. For three years, she had the honor of counseling women at the Truth Home, a residential treatment program for women who have been trafficked. Her experience also includes providing member care for missionaries around the world through Safe Place Ministry.

What is a faith-based healing group? What are the benefits of the healing group?

The Healing Wounds of Trauma (HWT) group provides a safe environment for people who have experienced heart wounds. A heart wound is another name for trauma.

Heart wounds affect every part of our lives. They affect our emotional, mental, physical, and spiritual being. The HWT introduces the hurting, grieving, and injured to healing power of the cross and the Scriptures.

This curriculum can be put into the hands of the church throughout the world. It is in 42 countries, on 5 continents, and translated into 157 languages. Also, it has brought healing to people incarcerated in several countries.

The beauty of the curriculum is that people who have experienced healing for the first time or received further healing desire to bring healing to those in their sphere of influence. Those that have the passion to facilitate healing groups can attend a training. This is a way for the healing to grow and provide healing in different churches, ministries, and organizations. The book is simple; however, the use of Scriptures and real conversation facilitate a healthy environment of safety and acceptance. Each lesson provides best mental health practices with the Bible to provide a place to heal from trauma. It is emphasized as a healing journey. It is personal and unique to each individual.

What are some of the best Scriptures from the Bible to help someone heal from trauma and abuse?

There are six core lessons ranging from "what is a heart wound" to "how can we forgive other."

Each lesson has specific Scriptures. Generally, each participant receives a book or Scripture handouts. The participants can review the Scriptures that best speak to their hearts. Trauma robs us of our voice, choice, and relationships. People have the opportunity to choose which lessons provide healing to their souls.

What's important for our readers to know about faith-based trauma healing groups?

What I have discovered is that Healing Wounds of Trauma-How the Church Can Help provides the space and time to talk about the "hard" things. Generally, certain topics are not discussed within the church. Most likely there are people sitting in the pews crying, if not screaming, inside themselves because they experienced horrible things and don't know how to talk about them nor what to do with them. They have been silenced without being told to be silent.

Some of the optional lessons are Domestic Abuse, Suicide, Addictions, Abortion, Rape and Sexual Assault, HIV/AIDS, and Moral Injury. When people are able to honestly share from their hearts about their thoughts of suicide, the years they witnessed domestic violence and then married into it, the sexual abuse they experienced by the person who is to love and protect them, and secretly live in an addiction, healing and love and acceptance are given within the group. Sometimes all someone needs to hear is, "Yea, me too." Some almost immediately break into praising God with tears streaming down their faces.

Church needs to be real and safe. Jesus always was. He knew how to approach someone with love and humility and provide the space and time to talk about the hard things that happen to us. Read and study Jesus in the Gospels. He demonstrates to us how to help others heal.

What resources do you recommend for individuals to heal from trauma?

- *When Dad Hurts Mom: Helping Your Children Heal the Wounds of Witnessing Abuse, Why Does He Do That?* By Lundy Bancroft
- *Redeeming Heartache How Past Suffering Reveals Our True Calling, Wounded Heart* by Dan Allender
- *The Soul of Shame, The Soul of Desire* by Curt Thompson, MD
- *When Loving Him is Hurting You* by Dr. David Hawkins
- *Is It Abuse: A Biblical Guide to Identifying Domestic Abuse & Helping Victims* by Darby Strickland
- *The Life-Saving Divorce* by Gretchen Baskerville
- *Try Softer* by Aundi Kolber
- *The Body Keeps the Score* by Bessel Van Der Kolk, MD
- Podcasts: "The Place We Find Ourselves" by Adam Young, "Allender Center Podcast" by Dan Allender, "In The Light" by Dr. Anita Phillips, "Being Known" by Curt Thompson, MD

~

Laura's Story

What was the most difficult part about living in a domestic violence relationship?

I think most women say it is the tension that exists while the anger and aggression build. You live in a constant state of anxiety. I had two very small children when I finally left, but I was also a nurse in the emergency department, and I didn't want anyone to know—not my family nor the people I worked with. I had no friends because he had systematically made it impossible to be with anyone due to his behavior especially when he drank. Alcohol was definitely a catalyst for the violence.

What was the most difficult part about leaving a domestic violence relationship?

The financial aspects of getting out. Being afraid I wouldn't be able to take care of my kids. He was self-employed so I almost had to pay him money, but in the end, I took nothing and started over from scratch to make sure my boys were safe. I would have slept in my car at that point because I was afraid that I would end up like Nichole Brown Simpson. At times I really feel like she saved my life. I left right after the OJ trial because I was terrified that I would be next, and no one cares if a woman dies.

What guidance would you give someone who is trying to leave or heal from it?

Therapy. I still to this day have PTSD. I think about how much it has affected my relationships and how I react even after years of trying to work on things.

It took me 24 years to get married again. I dated a man right after I got divorced and didn't trust enough that when he said he wanted to get married it was a real partnership with respect and caring. He wasn't insecure or controlling, but I got cold feet, even though I loved him with all my heart. So, the fear and anxiety created in my marriage prompted me not to trust and break up with him. I didn't speak to him for 18 years, but then I saw him at a funeral, he hugged me, and I married him a year later. I probably would not have trusted myself to make such a spontaneous decision if it had not been for therapy.

Also surround yourself with people who lift you up, not drag you down. People who are abused are typically givers and that can get physically and emotionally exhausting. Learn to say no and feel confident it wasn't because you couldn't help but maybe at that moment you just need to say no for self-preservation.

I hope this helps just one person.

~

Grant me the serenity to accept that which cannot be changed, the courage to change that which can be changed, and the wisdom to know the difference.

SIX

10 TIPS

We cannot force someone to hear a message they are not ready to receive. But we must never underestimate the power of planting a seed.

Every hardship in life offers an opportunity for transformation and growth. Here are 10 tips I've learned throughout my personal and professional experiences.

Tip 1: Believe in something bigger than yourself.

When you are living in a domestic violence home, where you feel like you are constantly walking on eggshells, you can reach a moment where you feel hopeless. Sometimes people reach a point where they don't know what else to do or say to try to fix their relationship. Where do you turn at that point?

Some people believe in a higher power. Others believe in trusting the universe.

I think we can struggle with this when we feel like our prayers might not be answered. Let's say we pray for our relationship to be healed or fixed, but it doesn't happen. Consider changing your prayer.

Maybe the prayer can become about giving you the strength to leave. Or maybe the prayer is about aligning you with resources to help you heal. I believe in the serendipitous moments that come into our paths. When I hear the same messages from individuals in different, unconnected places, I smile because I know it isn't coincidence that I am hearing the same message. It's a lesson. Something to ponder. Something to help me grow. I believe that we find ourselves in the same situations over and over again when there is a lesson that needs to be learned but we just haven't taken the time to learn it yet.

Tip 2: Learn to live in the present.

If the relationship that you were in was manipulative, you might feel the need to replay back all the things that happened to remind yourself that you aren't crazy. When the disrespect toward you was dismissed on a regular basis, you have to remind yourself of your worth. When I have spoken to people on their healing journey, they validate the need to replay what has happened and also offer some level of hope that you will reach a point where you feel like you no longer need to tell your story anymore. Maybe you feel like you finally made sense of what happened. Maybe you just get tired of talking about it.

As a therapist, I have felt, seen, and heard so much pain. I knew that I have the ability to speak up and offer another level of support to the community.

In therapy, I ask my clients to share about their past to help them understand how and why they are a certain way. Then we can go into the future and discuss what goals they would like to achieve.

I fully believe that the present moment is the best place to live. In the present moment, we can focus on what is going well here and now. If that moment feels difficult, you might have to really try to find any little thing to identify as positive. Not every day is good, but we can try to find something good in every day.

Beware of destination addiction, telling yourself that you will be happy when something happens, such as when you get a new car, different job, bigger home. It's important to learn how to see the happiness, contentment, and small moments of joy in your present daily life.

Tip 3: Journal to unload your mind for release and clarity.

Every day, I feel like I have a million and one thoughts going through my head: my to-do list, cleaning, errands, paperwork, phone calls, worries, fears, anxieties, relationships, goals, dreams. The list goes on and on. We only have 24 hours each day. Choose your direction wisely.

To unload your brain, I recommend journaling, such as:

- Free flow journaling or something that I learned about from a book called Clarity Cleanse. I would set a timer and write out all my thoughts, profanity and all, scribble it out messy, and then I would rip it up and burn it to ashes in a bucket in my backyard. It felt cleansing and therapeutic. That is probably my favorite type of journaling. You don't go back and read it. You just release it.
- I have also tried intentional journaling, writing about a specific stressor that I am going through in hopes that writing it out will provide clarity or answers.
- Another way that this can be more therapeutic is when I encourage my clients to write a letter to someone who they have unresolved emotions toward or words left unspoken. It can be helpful to write it out on paper instead of it cycling through your head.
- Then there is prompted journaling. These can be really fun. You can purchase journals in stores or online with specific themes or prompts. They tend to be really good for people interested in self-reflection
- Also consider keeping a daily gratitude journal.
- To take journaling one step further, consider looking into workbooks.

As you journal, feel free to feel your feelings. Allow yourself to feel all of it through your healing journey. Yes, it is messy, but there is beauty in that if we choose to see it.

Consider crying and viewing that action as cleansing. Where our society or even perhaps our family might lead us to believe that crying indicates weakness, I choose to have a different perception. Tears can be a sign of someone's courage, strength, and authenticity —for both women and men. There is healing power in crying and showing our emotions.

Tip 4: Shift your mindset with affirmations.

I have 2,039 affirmations on my phone. Every day, I either go on an app on my phone, scroll on Pinterest, or read a Scripture or from an affirmation book. Either way, it would always help my mind to shift in a healthier way, even if it was just for that moment.

I think we often underestimate the amount of control we have over our thoughts. We believe whatever we tell ourselves, whether it's true or false.

So, if we have the ability to tell ourselves what we want to believe, why not try to make it positive, kind, and loving. I have seen and encouraged people to also write positive "I am" statements on Post-it Notes to hang around their homes, in their car, at the office. You could even post an affirmation on your bathroom mirror. There are a lot of creative, fun ways to incorporate affirmations into your daily routine.

A positive affirmation a day can help to keep the unhealthy thoughts away. Reading daily affirmations has been a habit of mine for years. Whether it is reading from an app on my phone or from a book, it is a healthy routine that has never failed me.

Two apps that I enjoy using the most are the "I AM" and "Think Up" apps.

"I AM" are two of the most powerful words in the English language because whatever we say afterward can either lift us up or break us down, depending on what we choose to say to ourselves. Individuals will challenge me on this by asking, "All I have to do is repeat these to myself daily, and I will believe them?"

YES! Think about any habit that you ever tried to implement. After doing it over and over, it eventually became automatic. Now think about a negative, self-critical thought that you might have. For me, it's, "I'm not good enough." That is not always something that I believed about myself. I wasn't born with that thought in my head. At some point, I heard it from somewhere or had an interaction with someone that made me feel like I wasn't good enough. Then I thought about it so much that it became part of my automatic thought process. It's not true, but I repeated it so often that it became true.

This works then same way with positive thoughts. If you think something positive enough times, you will believe it.

What I appreciate about some of the apps available is that you can set alarms for them to automatically pop up on your phone screen. That still requires you to be intentionally enough to read them and actually let the words sink in.

I suggest using these apps before you get out of bed in the morning, right before you go to sleep, or both. It's not possible to use positive affirmations too much.

What I appreciate about the Think Up app is that you record your own voice to the affirmations that you choose, making these affirmations very personal. The important concept to remember here is that we believe what we tell ourselves, so choose wisely.

> *"Your thoughts become your words. Your words become your behavior. Your behavior becomes your habits. Your habits become your values. Your values become your destiny."*
> *—Mahatma Gandhi*

Here are some affirmations to get you started, from the I Am and the Motivation apps.

- Why give up on yourself? Instead prove the naysayers wrong, become the best version of yourself.
- You are powerful beyond measure, and new beginnings are making their way to you.
- I'm open to changing my beliefs in the face of new information.
- I remain centered and calm despite what's happening around me.
- Love yourself enough to live a healthy lifestyle.
- I am a positive being, aware of my potential.
- I love myself deeply and fully.
- Sometimes the hardest thing and the right thing are the same.
- I can grow healthy and strong by taking care of my body.
- Tomorrow allows new opportunities.
- Your biggest fear is also your biggest opportunity for growth.
- I open my heart to love, and I know that I deserve it.
- I am proud of the person that I am becoming.
- I love myself through tough times.
- My day is filled with potential for joy, love, and happiness.
- If you change the way you look at things, the things you look at change.
- I give myself permission to trust myself, my guidance, and my intuition.
- You cannot be broken. You cannot be defeated. This is your time to rise.
- I move toward situations that make my soul happy.
- Today I leave old habits in the dust where they belong.
- I will not let the dark times consume me
- I accept where I am in this point in my journey.
- I am filled with gratitude for the mentors showing up when I need them.

- I believe in myself relentlessly.
- Saying no to the wrong things makes space for the right things.
- I believe in my capabilities.
- I love myself, respect myself, and accept myself as I am."

Tip 5: Learn to say no and yes to set boundaries.

I define myself as a recovering people pleaser. I was definitely a yes person. At one point, I loved to be the yes person. I liked people to see me from the perspective of a woman who had it all together. I had my business, my marriage, my kids, and my volunteering. What I ended up noticing is how often I became depleted.

Then I read a book called *Breathing Room*. The author encourages you to identify all the things that you do on a regular basis and to also identify all the extra things that you commit to. Then you're encouraged to ask, out of all those lists, what are the commitments that you really enjoy? The barrier to getting rid of those commitments you don't enjoy is if you are a person who feels guilty when you say no.

An important thing to remember is that learning how to say no is setting a healthy boundary for yourself. There could be some people in your life who will continue to take from you as much as you are willing to give. Keep in mind balance. Keep in mind healthy give and take in a relationship or a team. All of the burden shouldn't always fall on the one same person. In a toxic or abusive relationship, you might feel in an almost constant state of depletion. You probably give a lot of yourself mentally and emotionally just trying to keep things together on a daily basis.

Remember to love yourself. If you spend so much of your time and energy trying to keep things as calm as possible at home and having things run as smooth as possible, you can become exhausted.

Parents, please try to be kind to yourself and remind yourself that self-care shows your children a healthy example to follow. Rather than choosing between exercising or spending time with your kids, why not exercise with your kids.

Tip 6: Don't take things personally.

One of my favorite tools to share is called the 4 Agreements by Don Miguel Ruiz. You'll find a vast amount of information in his book of the same name, and one of his four agreements that you make to yourself is don't take things personally. (The others are be impeccable with your word, don't make assumptions, and always do your best.) The truth is that nothing other people do is because of you. What others say and do is a projection of their reality, their dream. Once you become immune to the opinions of others, you will be free from much needless suffering.

When people respond in a way you dislike, remember that sometimes an individual's response or reaction to you has nothing to actually do with you. Sometimes it is showing you where their unresolved wounds are. It might help to learn to pray for them. We don't have the ability to help or heal anyone who isn't ready to help themselves. This is a lesson for many of us, but we tend to dig our heals in the ground and say, "I can do it. Let me just try one more thing." But at some point, I think we all reach a point where we had enough.

Tip 7: Find your true self.

We live in a very judgmental world, one that tells us how we are supposed to look, think, feel, act, eat, etc. I think perhaps the most difficult part of living in this world is learning how to be yourself without letting anyone make you feel like you aren't good enough because you don't fit in their mold. I imagine to a certain extent, we all want to feel approved of, validated, and liked by others.

What I have learned is the only thing that really matters is whether or not you love yourself. Are you proud of the person who you are? I'm a firm believer that the more time and energy that you put into healing, God or the universe will cross your path with other people who are on a healing journey as well.

How do we distinguish between our false self and true self. Consider this.

The false self is about our ego. These are qualities that I believe we can inherent because of our unhealthy family dynamic or society. These are some of those toxic belief systems that we can work on changing, including separation, blame, hostility, resentment, pride, complaining, jealousy, anger, power, materialism, war, intolerance, self-importance, self-denial, doing (rather than being), and anything else that focuses on "me"

I encourage you to live toward becoming your true self or what makes your soul feel good, such as unity, understanding, love, gratefulness, humbleness, spiritualism, wisdom, peace, empathy, altruism, self-acceptance, simplicity, being (rather than doing), and anything else that focuses on "we."

Tip 8: Find your voice and your tribe, including experts.

It might all come down to this one piece of advice: PLEASE don't ever allow a toxic person make you feel like your voice or story doesn't matter! They are trying to silence you for a reason because they don't want to address the problem. Even if other people choose not to acknowledge a major problem, it doesn't mean that you have to ignore it as well.

I believe that one of the reasons why we choose to not speak is because we don't want to feel shame. However, when shame is shared, cycles of victimhood are permitted to heal as you find the courage to speak your truth. Because abuse and neglect can only be perpetuated in silence, it is your willingness to step forward and share your story that helps to transform each wound and inspires others to be set free. Once your shame is shared, you are able to honor yourself with the heightened encouragement, worthiness, and validation that you deserve to receive.

Trauma survivors crave honesty and authenticity. They've had to fight for their ability to think clearly, and they know who they are. It costs you greatly. You aren't willing to engage with people who do not honor that.

Remember: You can be genuinely kind, loving, and considerate *and* still possess the power and ability to use your voice, stand in your truth, and let other people know when they messed up. Being kind does NOT equal being silenced and accepting other people's disrespect and poor behavior.

Tip 9: Understand the benefits of isolation and silence.

Before you argue with someone, ask yourself, *Is this person mentally mature enough to grasp the concept in a different perspective?* Sometimes it's important to speak up with your strength, but other times it's healthy to keep your strength inside for a while. You can and will learn how to discern which moments require which response.

Your direction is more important than your speed. So, if your healing journey requires you isolating for a while in order to achieve your inner peace, if it means removing commitments to your calendar, then do it.

In a world that is way too focused on social media, here are some healthy tips to consider.

- I am unplugging to unwind.
- I am spending less time scrolling and more time living.
- I don't need to know what everyone is doing, and they don't need to know everything that I am doing.
- Everything I do doesn't need to be seen or heard.
- Special time with myself is time well spent.
- I am posting less to do more.
- I can grow and glow privately.

I think our society puts too much emphasis on having to be in a relationship. Instead of putting so much time and effort into "finding the one," why not put your time and energy into "becoming the one." Being "single" shouldn't be frowned upon. Do you know what can happen when you choose to be single?

You can find yourself. You can heal yourself. You can love yourself. You can become passionate about your dreams. You can focus on your health and fitness. You can grow friendships. You can make new memories. And yes, you can do all of that in a relationship, too. But I think a common situation is we intentionally or unintentionally jump from one relationship to another because we don't want to feel the pain. We want to find the quickest way possible to fill the void.

Tip 10: Be in control and learn to let go.

When living with someone who struggles to manage their anger, you might feel like you are constantly walking on eggshells, being extra careful about everything that you say and do, anxious about what might happen if you slip up. The sad part about it is you never know what the trigger to someone's anger can be. As hard as you try, you are not in control of the situation. If you reach a point where you felt helpless, hopeless, and depleted, you might realize that the best thing you can do is to learn how to let go of your relationship. If you choose to let go, PLEASE be patient and kind with yourself. This is an unbelievably difficult journey to navigate.

Loving Kindness Meditation

May I be safe.

May I be happy.

May I be healthy.

May I live with ease.

—Lisa A. McCrohan

You can repeat this using any name, pronoun, or descriptor you like, such as "May you be safe." Or, "May my children be safe."

One fun way that you can try to pull all these tools together is to make yourself what I call a healing box. This can look similar to a calming toolkit for a child. If you are a parent, I encourage you to design these boxes with your child. If you or them are having a moment of struggle, you can grab your box. I have added to mine over the years. It includes things like putty, a fidget spinner, and a worry stone for when my anxiety is elevated. I also added healing mantra cards and prayer cards for when I want to shift my mind toward healing or strengthen my spirituality. I took a monthly yoga class where the instructor gave us stones and affirmation cards that were beautiful reminders of self-love and compassion, so I added them to my healing box.

One special thing that I think can be added are photos of yourself or your children. We transform during our healing, so taking photos of yourself to represent your moments of love, laughter, light are very important. I had actually won a free photo shoot last year, and my favorite prop was a sign that said, "I am worthy of love and respect."

Don't be afraid to start over. This time you're not starting from scratch, you are starting from experience.

SEVEN

POINTS TO PONDER

Now that you understand about the hidden wounds of abuse and the importance of speaking up and shifting old beliefs, here are some questions to think about and points to ponder. Let's dig a little deeper to better understand yourself.

Before passing judgment onto someone else, are you aware of your own wounds and experiences and how those might influence the way that you are viewing another person or their situation?

____

____

What could be an alternative perspective that you can have about this person or situation?

____

____

If the words you spoke appeared on your skin, would you still be beautiful?

If the world was blind, how many people would you impress?

Do your daily choices support the life you are trying to create for yourself?

What are your unmet needs?

What words or actions from others help to heal your soul?

How do you show yourself love on a daily basis?

What positive lessons do your actions show others in your home?

What can I do that will serve the greater good?

What can I do to serve life's deepest purpose?

Did I offer peace today?

Did I bring a smile to someone's face?

Did I say words of healing?

Did I forgive?

Did I love?

We are all one. It is only our egos and fears that separate us.

Once we better understand ourselves, we can better understand others.

What if every time we saw a child acting "defiant," we ask ourselves, "What need isn't being met for them?"

Now what if we applied that thought when we saw an *adult* acting defiant. "What need was unmet for them when they were a child—not heard, not seen, not loved."

What experience did this person have that caused them pain? Who taught or showed them that it was okay to then inflict their pain onto someone else?

How can we as a community show them a different path?

It's okay to have compassion for the abusers, too.

Maybe there might even be a time you want to thank the traumatic situation. Some traumatic situations are so painful, there is no way to find something good in them. There is no lesson. However, perhaps in the little "t" trauma events?

This might sound a little crazy, but hear me out.

When we shift from asking W*hy did this happen TO me* to *Why did this happen FOR me*, we can try to view things differently.

Where has it led me? What beauty has developed from that pain?

For me, I published a book. I'm invited to do speaking engagements. I'm developing a task force for our community. I'm getting certified to be a faith-based trauma healing group facilitator. Also, I'm trained to facilitate trauma groups for parents in schools. I'm connected with several amazing individuals and groups who are trauma-informed, faith-based, and helping our community.

My strength has grown.

My faith has grown.

The loving people in my life have grown.

Speaking up has aligned me with trauma-informed people and groups.

This provided me validation and healing in my journey.

I've felt seen, heard, valued, and understood—perhaps more than ever before—as my true self.

I see so much beauty and love here!

Learning to embrace all moments of our life is difficult. Trauma was part of your journey, but it doesn't necessarily define who you are as a person.

The trauma and abuse you experienced by someone else was NOT your fault.

However, the healing IS your responsibility.

It's absolutely difficult to navigate. But with healthy skills and healthy supports, you too, can pivot your pain into passion.

I believe in you!

There are points to ponder everywhere—in everything we see, hear, person we interact with, book we read, move we watch. Pause and take the time to notice the beautiful messages all around us for our healing.

A movie that was aligned with me is *Eat, Pray, Love*. I always have appreciation for expression of creativity. I think we all have favorite movies or songs that speak to us in moments of sadness, that get you lost in your heart and soul. I cried watching this movie many times. Then something beautiful happened during my healing journey. I watched this movie again, and I smiled. Here are a few quotes from the movie that spoke to me.

"We all want things to stay the same, to settle for living in misery because we are afraid of change and things crumbling to ruins… Ruin is a gift. Ruin is the road to transformation. We should always be prepared for endless waves of transformation."

"I know you feel awful, but your life is changing, and it's not a bad thing. If you miss him, then miss him. Send him some light and love every time you think of him then drop it. If you could clear out all that space in your mind that you use to obsess over things you can't change, you would have a vacuum with a doorway and do you know what the universe would do to that doorway? God would rush in and fill you with more love than you ever dreamed of. I think you have the capacity someday to love the whole world.

"Sometimes losing balance for love is part of living life. In the end, I've come to believe in something that I call the physics of the quest. A force in nature governed by laws as real as the laws of gravity. The rule of quest physics goes like this: If you are brave enough to leave behind everything familiar and comforting, which can be anything from your house, bitter old resentments, and set out on a truth-seeking journey, either externally or internally, and if you are truly willing to regard everything that happens to you on that journey as a clue. And if you accept everyone you meet along the way as a teacher. And if you are prepared, most of all, to face and forgive some really difficult realities to find yourself, then the truth will not be withheld from you. I can't help but believe it, given my experience."

~

Kim's Story

What was the most difficult part about living in a domestic violence relationship?

I think one of the most difficult things about living in a domestic violence situation was the stress and anxiety from the constant feeling that you are walking on eggshells. While there was no physical abuse in my personal situation, there was lots of mental/emotional abuse. There was a constant feeling of not wanting to do something "wrong" to keep the peace and avoid the put-downs that inevitably came with not following some rule or meeting some expectation that, at best, were ambiguous to start with. Even worse was the silent treatment, as if I was invisible and nonexistent. Another huge part that was very difficult was attempting to shield my three children from it.

What was the most difficult part about leaving a domestic violence relationship?

I think the most difficult part of leaving the relationship was the fear of the unknown. The dysfunction of living with it became so normal that the fear of having no idea what life on my own with my children would be like was huge. I was also very concerned about breaking up my family and what that would do to my children.

What guidance would you give to someone who is trying to leave or heal from it?

I have several pieces of advice that I would offer to people who are leaving a domestic violence relationship. First, build up a big support system with friends and family. You need to hear many times that you are making the best decision and not give into the temptation to go back. I also suggest getting an impartial therapist to help you work on yourself. I didn't realize how little I thought of myself and just how dysfunctional my relationship life was until I was on the other side of it. Finally, I would like others leaving domestic violence situations to know that while you think you were doing the right thing for your children by keeping the family together, it negatively impacts them so much more than you even realize. A dysfunctional, emotionally unhealthy marital relationship doesn't really end with a happy family, no matter how much we think we can make up for, cover up, or wish away.

~

"Don't just learn, also experience.
Don't just read, also absorb.
Don't just change, also transform.
Don't just relate, also advocate.
Don't just promise, also prove.
Don't just criticize, also encourage.
Don't just think, also ponder.
Don't just take also give.
Don't just see, also feel.
Don't just dream, also do.
Don't just hear, also listen.

> **Don't just talk, also act.**
> **Don't just tell, also show.**
> **Don't just exist, also live."**
> —Roy T. Bennett, *The Light in the Heart*

EIGHT

PIVOT YOUR PAIN INTO PASSION

Give. But don't allow yourself to be used.
Love. But don't allow your heart to be abused.
Trust. But don't be naive.
Listen. But don't lose your own voice.

Is it okay to wear rose-colored glasses? Yes, however, please don't forget to look over those lenses every once in awhile to consider a different and potentially healthier perspective that might provide you with an opportunity to learn and grow. In a harsh world, choose to be a person who sees the love! Choose to allow your challenges to not make you bitter, but better. Use your experiences, your lessons, and your voice to help yourself and others. I'm not sure any of us are ever fully healed. Maybe life is about us all being on a continuous healing journey together.

But what about imposter syndrome. You might wonder: *Who am I? What can I do? I'm not so special that I can make an impact.* Never underestimate the power of planting a seed.

Instead of living in resentment and anger, pivot your pain into passion. What does that mean? Think about all the time and energy you put into your anger and fighting. You could put that time and energy into something healthy that benefits yourself and others. How amazing would that be?!

One of the best books to align with at this time is *Change your World* by John Maxwell and Rob Hoskins.

As you let go of anger and embrace healing, never let go of hope.

"Hope has two beautiful daughters; their names are Anger and Courage: Anger at the way things are, and Courage to see that they do not remain as they are."
—Augustine of Hippo

The truth is there are problems that can use our help everywhere. If change is possible, then why aren't we doing more to change our world? The reality is that most of us are waiting for someone else to do something about the problems we see. But we can't always wait for change and be passive bystanders.

Transformation is possible for anyone willing to learn and live good values, value people, and collaborate with others to create a positive values culture.

"Optimism is the belief that things will be better. Hope is the faith that, together, we can make things better."
—Jonathon Sacks

It takes a great deal of courage to have hope.

We can make excuses, or we can make change. People change for some of these reasons: When they hurt enough that they have to change, when they see enough that they are inspired to change, or when they learn enough that they want to change. Change spreads from me to we when we are surrounded by people who want to make a difference. Abuse and trauma shouldn't have to *happen* to you in order for it to *matter* to you.

As a licensed therapist seeing the incidence of trauma increase, I would love to see more change.

One way that change can occur is by connecting with other people in your community. I recently had the privilege of being invited to attend a TREE training through United Way and Resilient Lehigh Valley. TREE stands for Trauma, Restorative practices, Emotional Intelligence, and Equity. It has by far been one of the most beautiful trainings that I ever attended. The facilitators and participates showed transparency, vulnerability, and an overall desire to learn how to heal ourselves as well as educate others in our community. Trauma is difficult work, there is no doubt about it. I have a high level of respect for individuals who go through the journey of healing. And for those who haven't figured out how to heal yet, please know that you aren't alone. If there is one thing that I have learned through my own healing journey is once we choose that we will be determined to heal, no one can stop us. We have the ability to break the cycle. And on that journey of becoming your true self, your path will cross with other individuals who are also on a healing journey and you will never feel alone again. You will be reminded in every interaction that you are seen, heard, and valued and isn't that what we all deserve? Together we can show each other how to remove the shame, judgement, and criticism and lead each other with compassion, understanding, and kindness.

One message that the facilitator emphasized in TREE training is how much our stories matter. So, then another way that I pivoted my pain into passion was writing this book. I had received many serendipitous signs from people that encouraged me to put pen to paper and fingers to keys to write and publish the book that you are holding. To think that if I listened to the people in the beginning of my healing journey who told me to stop speaking, this never would have come to fruition. This is a reminder that we are stronger than we think.

Focusing more on we than me, I began speaking to others about creating a domestic violence task force for the community I live in.

Lehigh Valley Domestic Violence Task Force

Mission statement: The Lehigh Valley Domestic Violence Task Force will create and implement a three-year strategic planning process. Our aim is to decrease the impact domestic violence has on families and systems in our community.

Schools, hospitals, health and human service providers, county, police departments, and the court system will coordinate services. Within our service sectors, our aim is to identify families and plan for safety. As a collaborative, we will support family achievement of healthy lives.

Vision Statement: Heal our families. Heal our community.

Goals:

1. Evaluate stakeholders' awareness of domestic violence and safety net resources
2. Collect screening tools and methods that identify signs of domestic violence
3. Identify evidence-based, trauma-informed strategies currently in place
4. Collect and discuss prevention and intervention statistics by service sector
5. Design and enact a three-year plan to decrease the risk factors and increase the protective factors among families impacted by domestic violence
6. Annually report the incidence of domestic violence in Northampton County over the three years

Objectives:

- Define a baseline measure
- Identify protocols, screening tools, assessments, treatment, and resources for families
- Identify services inventory by supplier and supplier availability

- Identify all evidence-based services and service availability
- Document requirements for exchange of information/confidentiality
- Identify subcommittees, responsibilities, prevention, and intervention plans
- Define success measures

Whether developing a task force or finding your tribe, consider who you want to invite to your table. Someone who:

- Understands the value of questions
- Desires the success of others
- Adds value to other's thoughts
- Is not threatened by other's strengths
- Can emotional handle changes
- Understands their place and value at the table
- Brings out the best in people around them
- Has a "we" and not "me" attitude

What could you do to pivot your pain into passion?

- Perform random acts of kindness
- Start a support group
- Obtain a certification in an area that you would like to guide others to heal in

"When we find the courage to use our voice, it has the power to positively inspire or change the lives of others. It's part of the special gift you have to offer the world and is something to be cherished and championed, never hidden."
—Nicole O'Neill

HEALING RESOURCES

Organizations

- ACEs Connection Resource Center
- One Mom's Battletina@tinaswithin.com
- Pennsylvania Coalition Against Domestic Violence (PACDV)
- Resilient Lehigh Valley

Books

- *Change Your World: How Anyone, Anywhere Can Make a Difference,* by John Maxwell and Rob Hoskins
- *The Whole-Brain Child Workbook: Practical Exercises, Worksheets and Activities to Nurture Developing Minds* by Daniel Siegel J Daniel, MD
- *Thriving as an Empath* by Judith Orloff, MD
- *Love Yourself, Heal Your Life Workbook* by Louise Hays
- *The Energy Bus* by Jon Gordon
- *Divine Beauty* by Michelle Cox and Jenn Gotzon

- *Journey to the Heart* by Melody Beattie
- *Set Boundaries, Find Peace* by Nedra Glover Tawwab
- *Radical Acceptance* by Tara Brach
- *Breathing Room Devotional* by Sandra Stanley
- *I Thought It Was Just Me* by Brene Brown, PhD

EPILOGUE

This book is based upon my education and experiences. I have presented tips here as options. My perspective is not the only way.

The information in the book can be heavy. I encourage you to take breaks, deep breaths, and time to process. This is not easy as most healing journeys are challenging, but please know this book was written from a place of love and my hope is that every reader can have the ability to hear my heart in it. I believe that our healing journeys are endless because we are all lifelong students. Please try to be patient and kind to yourself as you take that next small step forward. And know that you are never alone. Someone is praying and wanting the best for you at this very moment.

I encourage you to keep asking questions, lean into difficult conversations, and never stop learning. For more information, reach out to me (contact me through my profile on Victoria Alercia Counseling Services on www.psychologytoday.com) or find an expert or reliable resource.

ACKNOWLEDGMENTS

To my childhood lifelong friends—Jen, Ana, and Tina—without you, I don't know how'd I'd make it through some of these challenging moments in life. Thanks also to some of new friends whose paths have aligned with me during my healing over the last year—Amy and Susan—who also help in reminding me that it takes time to heal from trauma and allow me to speak as long as I need to.

Pastor Eric, Jane, Maria, Kathy, Janet, and the whole Gate family, thank you for always providing a genuine, safe, loving environment, to hold space for me, and to pray for me and with me.

To my spiritual advisor Kim, who has been on the healing journey with me for the past few years, through the messy times and the beautiful moments, always reminding me that I am stronger than I think and always loved by God, thank you.

A big thank you to Dr. Aaron, Reverend Lyn, and all of the experts in my book for sharing your education, experience, and beautiful guidance in healing.

Thank you to Dr. Lyz and the Visionistas team, who came into my life at the perfect time and reminding me that love can heal.

Thank you to the people who are developing the domestic violence task force with me. With your hope and strength, I have no doubt that we will provide healing in our community.

To the staffs at Turning Point, BW Nice, and other local organizations who continue to share their voices, stories, and missions to guide people affected by domestic violence to healing. Thank you for providing me the opportunity to share my voice as well.

Thanks to my publisher Jenn for being part of my healing journey, by believing in my vision, helping me to tell my story, and assisting me in bringing my book to life.

To God: Without you, none of this would be possible. I will continue to move forward, making choices fueled by love.

A huge thank you to my parents for providing a safe landing pad for me and my children as we were healing. Especially my mom, thank you for being our rock and always going above and beyond to take care of us.

And thank you to my children, who are always my reason for working so hard at my healing and helping others, to try to make a beautiful world for them to grow up in.

ABOUT THE AUTHOR

Victoria Alercia, LPC, is a licensed professional counselor with 15 years of experience in the mental health field. After filing for divorce last year, she chose to focus on her healing journey. This led her to combining her two passions: therapy and spirituality. She was recently trained with Resilient Lehigh Valley to facilitate the TREE program (trauma, restorative practices, emotional intelligence, equity). She is also working on becoming certified to facilitate faith-based trauma healing groups. She is currently offering two programs:

- I Am Loving the Me That I'm Choosing to Be, which is a free program to educate children in schools on how to develop a healthy mindset
- A New You, a program offered at Visionistas By Design to assist women on their healing journey after leaving an abusive relationship.

Victoria's podcast on YouTube offers many suggestions for education and community connections. She is dedicating much of her time and effort toward advocating for people who have been affected by domestic violence by sharing this book, scheduling speaking engagements, and developing a domestic violence task force for the Lehigh Valley.

For more information or to contact Victoria via phone or email, search for her profile on www.psychologytoday.com.